Praise for *Spinning Wyrd*

"This book is a journey of exploration throug.. ... cosmos as seen with Norse Pagan eyes. Ryan Smith invites the reader to encounter the living forces and beings that move through and animate all the Nine Worlds and to seek wisdom and relationship with each. But perhaps this book's most powerful offering is its insightful framework for understanding our own souls and our interactions with the forces that shape our fates. It's a compass that Norse-centered animists, polytheists, and Pagans can turn to for guidance along the path."

—Morpheus Ravenna, author of *The Magic of the Otherworld*

"*Spinning Wyrd* is the perfect follow-up to *The Way of Fire and Ice*, taking readers further into the ideas of radical Heathenry in ways that are both thought provoking and practical. Those seeking a Heathenry that is open and diverse, is strongly rooted in history but meant for today, and seeks to connect practitioners not only to gods but also to the many powers around us—understood through animism—will appreciate the way this book balances so many potentially conflicting things to form a cohesive whole. I loved the way Smith tackles potentially difficult topics like ecstatic practice with ease, both explaining why engaging with the more esoteric side of Heathenry is important and providing a guide for anyone to do so."

—Morgan Daimler, author of *Pantheon—The Norse and Pagan Portals—Odin*

"With this important book Ryan Smith has wrapped 'round our spindles the gift of theology about wyrd that is both rigorous and easily accessible: an animist understanding of the interconnectedness between all beings that better connects us to the ancestors we are always being born from and the futures that are always coming into being. *Spinning Wyrd* is an understanding of the cosmology of the Nornir that meets the contemporary moment and equips us with timeless mystic and ecstatic technologies to more prefigure the mutuality and pluralism we need in our worlds."

—Camellia-Berry Grass, devotional polytheist and author of *Hall of Waters*

"*Spinning Wyrd* is warm fire and glistening ice. Ryan Smith is somehow able to take extremely subtle concepts like wyrd and ørlog and explain them thoroughly, with practical applications, and even manages to connect them to political and social theory. This book is a must read for any Heathen seeking to dive deeper and learn how to work with the subtlest energies at play in the mundane and spirit realms."

—Siri Vincent Plouff, host of *The Heathen's Journey Podcast*,
coauthor of *Lessons from the Empress*

"*Spinning Wyrd* carefully and consciously helps readers deepen their practice amid challenging times. With the premise of Radical Heathenry, this inclusive book widens the view of Norse Paganism by looking at the often hard-to-grasp wyrd, amongst other significant concepts. Informed by extensive research, well-developed modern practices, and a commitment to social justice, this book prepares readers for whatever is fated to happen next."

—Irisanya Moon, author of *Pagan Portals—The Norns*

"As the leading voice for inclusive Heathenry, Smith presents an essential work exploring the cosmology and mysteries that lie at the heart of contemporary Heathen practice. Thorough yet approachable, *Spinning Wyrd* provides a solid framework for the new or practicing Heathen to uncover profound meaning and spiritual growth within their practice."

—Althaea Sebastiani, author of *Paganism for Beginners*

"[Smith's] is a tradition in which consent and respect for human and other-than-human people are rightfully emphasized on both mundane and magical levels. More importantly, though, *Spinning Wyrd* reminds us of our place within that ever-changing web [of wyrd], our responsibilities to our fellow people within it, and the power we hold to weave wisely for a better future. A perfect read for those looking to learn more about fire and ice Heathenry and its unique, socially / wyrd-conscious approach to magic!"

—Cat Heath, author of *Elves, Witches & Gods*

SPINNING
Wyrd

About the Author

Ryan Smith has been a practicing Pagan since his teens with over fifteen years of experience in inclusive and antiracist Heathen spirituality. He is the author of *The Way of Fire and Ice: The Living Tradition of Norse Paganism* and has contributed to the anthologies *Bringing Race to the Table: Exploring Racism in the Pagan Community* and *¡No Pasarán!: Antifascist Dispatches from a World in Crisis*. He has also been published at Huginn's Heathen Hof, Patheos Pagan, and Truthout and has presented talks and rituals at Pantheacon, the Gathering Paths presented by Between the Veils, Hexenfest, and Many Gods West. Ryan regularly writes at onblackwings.com and is currently producing a Heathen podcast, the *Wayward Wanderer*, which is available wherever you get your podcasts. He has a PhD in modern economic and social history and can be found online on Facebook, Mastodon, and Instagram.

A JOURNEY THROUGH THE
NORDIC MYSTERIES

SPINNING
Wyrd

RYAN SMITH

LLEWELLYN PUBLICATIONS
WOODBURY, MINNESOTA

FIRST EDITION
First Printing, 2023

Cover design by Shannon McKuhen
Interior art by the Llewellyn Art Department

Llewellyn Publications is a registered trademark of Llewellyn Worldwide Ltd.

Library of Congress Cataloging-in-Publication Data
Names: Smith, Ryan, author.
Title: Spinning Wyrd : a journey through the Nordic mysteries / Ryan Smith.

Description: First edition. | Woodbury, MN : Llewellyn Publications, a
    division of Llewellyn Worldwide Ltd, 2023. | Includes bibliographical
    references and index. | Summary: "Expanding on the radically inclusive
    practices presented in *The Way of Fire and Ice*, this next-step book
    teaches you how to tap into the forces of the Nordic cosmos. The
    greatest of these forces is wyrd, the symphony of life cocreated by the
    actions of all beings, from the humblest plants to the mightiest gods"—
    Provided by publisher.
Identifiers: LCCN 2023008478 (print) | LCCN 2023008479 (ebook) | ISBN
    9780738769851 | ISBN 9780738769950 (ebook)
Subjects: LCSH: Neopaganism—Scandinavia. | Mythology, Norse. | Gods,
    Norse. | Goddesses, Norse.
Classification: LCC BP605.N46 S64 2023 (print) | LCC BP605.N46 (ebook) |
    DDC 299/.940948—dc23/eng/20230308
LC record available at https://lccn.loc.gov/2023008478
LC ebook record available at https://lccn.loc.gov/2023008479

Llewellyn Publications
A Division of Llewellyn Worldwide Ltd.
2143 Wooddale Drive
Woodbury, MN 55125-2989
www.llewellyn.com

Printed in the United States of America

ALSO BY RYAN SMITH

The Way of Fire and Ice: The Living Tradition of Norse Paganism

CONTENTS

FIGURES

RITES AND EXERCISES

ACKNOWLEDGMENTS

This book would not have been possible without my partner Patricia's love and support. I could not have done it without you.

I further want to thank all my interview subjects for their participation and cooperation. Your words help root this book in living practice.

I also want to thank Elysia, Stephanie, and the rest of the Llewellyn editing team for your patience with my original draft and for sticking with this as the work emerged.

I additionally want to thank everyone who has ever jumped onto the Fire and Ice group, server, and study sessions. Your experiences and questions have fed every part of this book. That community would not be possible without all the generous people who have helped moderate those spaces, lead ritual, and keep this community together through thick and thin.

Finally, I dedicate this book to all the practitioners, mystics, wanderers, and others who find guidance and direction from this work. May this give you solace in the trying times we have been fated to experience.

INTRODUCTION

At Ithavoll met the mighty gods,
Shrines and temples they timbered high;
Forges they set, and they smithied ore,
Tongs they wrought, and they fashioned.
—Voluspo 7, *Poetic Edda*[1]

In a tattoo parlor, a practitioner lies beneath a needle infusing sacred motifs and runic patterns into their skin as they ride the pain of the moment to greater understanding. A maker sings songs of power into their latest creation, imbuing it with mystically crafted purpose and potential to alter reality on many levels. On the other side of the world, a ritualist inscribes bindrunes of justice over the latest construction notices posted at the edge of a dwindling, vibrant stretch of bayou. A mystic finds themself dancing in snow-crisp air to a melody ringing at the edges of their senses, seeking answers on a tide of ecstasy that follows. All are tapping into the forces of the Nordic cosmos, the greatest of which is wyrd.

---

1. All passages from the *Poetic Edda* quoted in this book are from Henry Adams Bellows, trans., *The Poetic Edda: The Mythological Poems* (Mineola, NY: Dover Publications, 2004).

Wyrd is the symphony of life cocreated by the actions of all beings, from the humblest living things to the mightiest of the godly and animistic Powers of Nordic practice. Listening to the melodies throughout the cosmos opens the way to a deeper understanding of life and the world around you. These forces define all of existence for the pre-Christian Nordic peoples and modern practitioners alike. Even gods are subject to these forces, as shown in their own shrines raised for unnamed purposes, hinting at mysteries dancing at the limits of their mighty wisdom. This book's goal is to help practitioners better understand these greater mysteries.

In Fire and Ice practice, these broader frameworks, which include animism, the nature of the individual, the World Tree, wyrd, the Norns, and Ragnarök, are fundamental to contemporary, revivalist practice. Developing a greater comprehension of how these greater forces work changes how you view the Powers and live your life on every level. These ideas are also essential for developing skill in the deeper forms of mysticism associated with Radical Heathenry.

Introducing Radical Heathenry

Radical Heathenry, also known as Fire and Ice Heathenry, is a form of Revivalist Nordic Paganism that is rooted in honoring the Powers of pre-Christian Nordic spirituality. It began as a set of practices that developed over the course of several years by Heathens living in northern California. It has since grown into a vibrant, inclusive spiritual tradition. Its core beliefs and practices are laid out in my book *The Way of Fire and Ice.*

At the core of Radical Heathenry are five points that set it apart from other forms of Heathen practice and define every aspect of this form of spirituality. These are living tradition, inspired adaptation, modern relevance, inclusive practice, and active involvement. Living tradition asserts that our practices are always growing and changing to best meet the needs of the practitioners in facing the challenges of the world we live in. Inspired adaptation argues that surviving source material such as the Eddas and historical sources are a starting point for developing practice and not the be-all and end-all of what can be done in Heathenry. Modern relevance claims spiritual practices and developments should find ways to be relevant for practitioners in the here and now and adapt to present conditions while retaining the core source of inspiration that makes it Heathen. Inclusive practice is the principle that all people are welcome to practice regardless of race, gender, sexuality, nationality, ability, or gender identity, and people advocating for bigoted ideologies should be actively excluded due to the harm they cause and represent. Active involvement accepts that spiritual practice permeates all aspects of life and should inspire us to take actions that make the world a better place.

The source of inspiration for this practice is pre-Christian Nordic spirituality as described in surviving source materials. These are the *Poetic Edda* and *Prose Edda*, historical sagas such as the Saga of the Icelanders and the Heimskringla, Nordic Scandinavian folklore, and the experiences of modern practitioners. Using this combination of sources provides rich material for developing all aspects of spiritual practice.

My introductory book, *The Way of Fire and Ice: The Living Tradition of Norse Paganism*, was a toolkit for developing personal and communal Norse spirituality, whether you practice on your own, are with a community, or are trying to start your own community. This sequel, *Spinning Wyrd*, is as much a toolkit as it is a philosophical work.

Mystically inclined practitioners will find a thorough set of tools for developing direct relationships with animistic Powers, communing with the dead, and cultivating their skills in ecstatic trance journeywork. You will find many examples in this book of how core concepts in Nordic Paganism interact with and sometimes clash with the assumptions of modern life.

All the material presented here is suitable for solitary and group practice with the intent of being as adaptable and inclusive to the widest range of potential needs. How you apply the ideas and methods presented here is entirely up to what you think works best for you.

A Bit about Me

I began my journey in Radical Heathenry without setting out to make a new form of Heathen practice. My friends and I got started because we were seeking an inclusive, more directly relevant yet authentic form of Heathen practice. Over the course of years, the members of the Golden Gate Kindred experimented with new ways of doing familiar rituals while also deconstructing or removing more bigoted elements of practice. We also agitated for more inclusive practice throughout Heathenry as part of Heathens United Against Racism.

All of these ideas were first brought together in my first book, *The Way of Fire and Ice*. This introductory book covers the core elements of Radical Heathen practice like the Nordic gods, the Nine Worlds, ethics, and ritual with introductory materials on ecstatic practice and the Nordic mystical practice known as modern seiðr (Heathen mysticism and magic). It also includes information on community organizing, providing seekers with all the tools they need to start their individual, group, and community practice.

I planned on writing a book on these topics as my first sequel to *The Way of Fire and Ice*, and the COVID-19 pandemic gave that project a further sense of urgency. I wanted to follow my first book with this one because I feel the cosmology and nature of reality in Heathenry are the most important aspects of this form of practice. Many people, I feel, first associate many forms of Pagan and Heathen practice with worshipping many gods. In Nordic myth, there are forces that are greater than the gods and these forces influence everything on every level of existence. These mightier forces, comparable to gravity and magnetism, are what truly makes Fire and Ice practice and inclusive Nordic forms of spirituality tick.

I also felt this would be a good place to further explore the practice of utiseta, one of the three forms of modern seiðr. Utiseta is a form of trance meditation where the practitioner uses this altered state for seeking guidance or finding answers. It is one of the more adaptable and accessible forms of seiðr and is a very useful tool for practitioners looking to go deeper. All the exercises in this book will help further develop your skills in this mystical art.

How to Use This Book

This book will work through the mysteries over the next seven chapters. Chapter 1 will begin the journey with further information and discussion of the ecstatic state and other, similar altered states of consciousness along with reenchantment and synchronicity, two concepts that are critical for understanding modern Heathen and Pagan philosophy.

Chapter 2 will explore wyrd, which is also commonly referred to as fate, and delve into the Norns. Chapter 3 zeroes in on the personal, discussing the four-part Nordic Self and what this means for the modern practitioner.

Chapter 4 will circle back to the greater cosmos by exploring Yggdrasil (the World Tree), the Nine Worlds sustained by its branches, and more information on utiseta journeywork. Chapter 5 will cover many beings of Nordic animism and contains the accounts of modern practitioners on animistic philosophy along with some rites and specific spiritual practices related to animism.

Chapter 6 will then travel from these living spirits of place to the deceased, the Nordic forms of necromantic mysticism, and the Nordic understanding of death that will also be supported by the accounts of modern Heathen practitioners. Chapter 7 brings all these strands together through the core rhythms seen in the great march from fire and ice pouring into the Ginnungagap to the cataclysm of Ragnarök and beyond.

Each chapter concludes with an exercise that builds on the information discussed in its associated chapter and some have examples of rites and bindrunes where relevant. Appendix I includes some of the exercises from *The Way of Fire and Ice* that are also used in the exercises in this book. Appendix II gives a brief overview of the sagas, myths, and translations used throughout this book.

Whether you are new to this practice or experienced, this book offers more for understanding several key concepts in modern Nordic cosmology. It will also help you deepen your understanding of modern Nordic mystical practices. I hope this book adds more to your personal practice and deepens your understanding of modern Nordic Paganism.

chapter one
RHYTHMS OF REALITY

A measure of wisdom each [person] shall have,
But never too much let [them] know;
Let no [one] the fate before [them] see,
For so they are freest from sorrow.
—HAVAMAL 56, *POETIC EDDA*

To begin our journey, three essential concepts need to be more fully examined: the ecstatic state, reenchantment, and synchronicity. The ecstatic state is a form of altered state of consciousness that can be reached using a variety of methods, and its use is very common in Fire and Ice practice. Reenchantment is the process of finding ways to infuse our, at times, overwhelmingly mundane world with a fresh sense of wonder, awe, and beauty. Synchronicity refers to a phenomenon when largely internal experiences such as dreams or visions during meditation and trance correspond with seemingly coincidental events in the material world.

All these concepts are often discussed in modern Pagan practices, providing a key framework for truly understanding and articulating what these ideas mean for the everyday practitioner. Each is essential for better comprehending the very different, at times utterly alien, worldview that comes with Nordic cosmology.

Understanding reenchantment and synchronicity will also help open the deeper layers of potential that come with modern Pagan and Heathen practice. This is owing to how all forms of modern Pagan and Heathen practice are as much lived, dynamic sets of experiences as they are ideas that are believed, rituals that are honored, and motions conducted to show participation in a shared spiritual culture. Everything is deeply connected to and in relationship with everything else in existence. These ties manifest in a whole host of different ways, some of which are more subtle or mysterious than others. These three ideas provide the keys to greater understanding of both Fire and Ice spirituality and your own relationships with the world around you.

Developing Ecstatic Practice

Altered states of consciousness, also known as ecstatic states, are a critical component of Fire and Ice spiritual practice. These states are used to help understand mythic concepts, cultivate relationships with the world around you, and shift your awareness from the ordinary to the otherworldly. Cultivating a better understanding of this state will help you develop your own spiritual practice and hone your skills with specific trance-heavy forms of Nordic mysticism such as deathwork and utiseta journeywork. The specifics of how you do this, in Fire and Ice practice, can be understood in terms of the kind of altered experience you are pursuing, which is referred to as Up or Down; how you use this shift in consciousness, referred to as In or Out; and the specific methods used in an ecstatic practice, which are known as processes and triggers.

The first of these core concepts that needs further explanation is Up or Down. An Upward oriented ecstatic state is where the practitioner achieves altered consciousness through conscious, engaged interaction with the world around them. Though this may sound strange and inaccessible, many people have already experienced Upward trances in their lives. Activities such as intense dancing, live musical performances, and playing in physical sports can induce feelings of time moving slowly and a sense of oneness with the people around them. Religious practices such as Sufi dervishes, Pentecostal Christian rites of speaking in tongues, Voudon dances, and the historic Dionysian revels can all be seen as examples of Upward trances. The Nordic peoples may have engaged in similar practices, such as those of the famed berserker cults and as part of more intense workings of seiðr sorcery along with well-documented folk dances associated with various harvest festivals throughout the year.

Downward ecstatic states, by contrast, are rooted in drawing your awareness and focus into yourself and away from the world around you. This shift in focus changes how you process information and understand life experiences. Sensory deprivation, such as draping a cloak over your eyes or going into a quiet, remote place, is a common tool in Downward ecstatic practices. Most forms of Downward-oriented ecstatic states are based in meditative practice of some kind or another, though not all Downward trances are necessarily meditative ones. Utiseta is the best example of Downward-based ecstatic practices from the Nordic peoples and provides a firm foundation for some of the more specialized branches of Nordic mysticism.

These pathways are used to help reach a specific direction, which is described as In versus Out. Inward ecstatic states focus on your resolving internal questions and concerns. Lucid dreaming and shadow work in witchcraft are excellent examples of an Inward-directed trance. Working with your fylgja is a similar example of an Inward trance in Fire and Ice practice and is described more in chapter 3. The Calming the Sea and Sky exercise in appendix I is another good example of a practice meant to induce such an ecstatic state. Inward trances invite introspection, self-examination, and resolution of your most deeply held concerns.

Outward trances, by contrast, focus on projecting your awareness beyond your form and into contact with the Powers and the Otherworlds. An Outward ecstatic state focuses on reaching sources of information that lie outside of your Self. Practices such as astral travel, channeling, and forms of possessory work can all be described as Outward-oriented trances. Utiseta journeywork and utiseta deathwork are two examples of Outward-oriented ecstatic practices that will be discussed further in chapters 4 and 6.

All forms of ecstatic practice in Fire and Ice Heathenry are a combination of both forms of measurement. How this works is illustrated in the following chart with specific examples:

UP

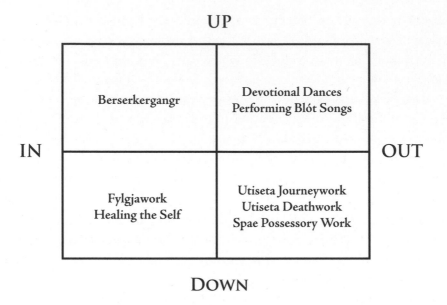

IN

Berserkergangr

Devotional Dances
Performing Blót Songs

Fylgjawork
Healing the Self

Utiseta Journeywork
Utiseta Deathwork
Spae Possessory Work

OUT

DOWN

Figure 1. Forms of Trance in Fire and Ice

These directional orientations give a sense of *how* you reach an ecstatic state with specific examples, but they do not answer the *what* of reaching altered states of consciousness. This is where processes and triggers come in. These terms refer to specific actions and sequences of actions you use to shift your consciousness into the ecstatic state. Processes and triggers, like Up versus Down and In versus Out, are often used as part of a broader process that integrates multiple actions. One particular benefit of using these tools consciously is you can use combinations of specific processes and specific triggers for inducing specific kinds of ecstatic states.

Processes are ritualized sequences of action that communicate to your conscious mind that you are actively shifting your consciousness. What these do is provide your more logical, material-oriented parts of the mind with an acceptable explanation for why your consciousness is about to shift. Processes can be as simple or elaborate as you like. All the meditative exercises included in this book and *The Way of Fire and Ice* are all processes that, through specific imagery and associations, ease your conscious mind into an altered, ecstatic state.

Triggers are specific, individual actions that interact with one of your five senses. These actions help change how you perceive the world, and using specific triggers as part of ecstatic practice helps create an association with that trigger and the ecstatic state. Things such as playing or singing specific songs, lighting incense, using candles, and hiding your eyes under a cloak or blindfold are excellent examples of triggers.

Triggers also reinforce associations between specific processes and specific uses of the ecstatic state. Utilizing specific triggers makes it easier to enter a desired ecstatic state and can help prevent practitioners from accidentally slipping into a different kind of trance than what they were originally preparing for or expecting.

Reenchantment

Such shifts in consciousness come with shifts in how you understand the world, with reenchantment being one of the most significant of these. Reenchantment is the argument and perspective the modern world has, in its pursuit of wealth and material accumulation, effectively stripped life of any sense of greater wonder and mystery, creating a state known as disenchantment.

Disenchantment is often connected to industrialization, though this concept is not, originally, a Pagan one. This concept, according to literary scholar Sara Lyons, can be traced back to German sociologist Max Weber's famous phrase "disenchantment of the world" from his 1918 "Science as a Vocation" lecture.[2] Many sources that deal with disenchantment focus most on the crowding out of religion and the otherworldly from social life.

This disenchantment is also tied to the tumult of this transformative period by Pagans, though this understanding tends to be far more visceral. Druid John Beckett provides an excellent example of a generally Pagan description of what disenchantment is and how it began. For Beckett, industrialization brought about disenchantment through its reshaping of natural landscapes, resulting in mass disconnection from the natural world. This effectively severed these age-old relationships, inflicting lasting trauma on the survivors and their descendants. He argues this is furthered by the modern world's tendency to work harder and consume more. For Beckett, disenchantment's dynamic of socially

---

2. Sara Lyons, "The Disenchantment/Re-Enchantment of the World: Aesthetics, Secularization, and the Gods of Greece from Friedrich Schiller to Walter Pater," *The Modern Language Review* 109, no. 4 (October 2014): 873–76, doi:10.5699/modelangrevi.109.4 .0873.

enforced disconnection from nature both is a product of the social processes that created our consumerist society and depends on the problem being consistently denied by calling for even more of what brought you there.[3]

Such a visceral understanding has roots in the violence associated with the rise of modern capitalism and industrialization. Beginning with the enclosure of the commons, the Trans-Atlantic slave trade, and colonialism and genocide in the Americas, the rise of this new world order depended on brutal applications of force to be realized. This cruel streak of dehumanization carried itself further into the newly created slums and the Dickensian factories. All these actions were made worse by the religious fervor invoked to justify mass dispossession, initiating what Cat Heath describes as an all-consuming religious war of conquest on an unprecedented scale.[4] Many of the ills and their fruits are still with us either in their consequences or in places where such abuses reign freely. When taken in this context, it makes sense why disenchantment can be seen as a form of lingering, unresolved cultural and social trauma.

Disenchantment in our present moment in history is one of the many symptoms of how the institutions born from these historical processes influence modern society's thinking. As Beckett argues, this process of disenchantment requires a constant feed of denial by using more products, more work, and more immiseration to sustain. As Beckett makes clear, he is not claiming this suggests your thoughts shape your reality; it does suggest disenchantment is a by-product of the constant drumbeat of "hustle, consume, repeat, until you die and face judgment" mentality that pervades every nook and cranny of society.[5]

For Heath, these accumulated harms are all part of a much broader struggle that she describes as "the fight in this land—the back and forth of Christians driving out the Other (both Human and non-Human) in order to maintain their damned, blood-soaked covenant."[6] The grinding effects of living in a wonderless, disconnected world are inescapable for all of us, manifesting as everything

---

3. John Beckett, "4 Steps to Re-enchant the World," Patheos Pagan, September 3, 2015, https://www.patheos.com/blogs/johnbeckett/2015/09/4-steps-to-re-enchant-the-world.html.

4. Cat Heath, "Restoration, Not Reenchantment," *Seo Helrune* (blog), October 29, 2018, https://seohelrune.com/2018/10/29/restoration-not-reenchantment/.

5. Beckett, "4 Steps to Re-enchant the World."

6. Heath, "Restoration, Not Reenchantment."

from health crises to substance abuse and worse for those deemed sufficiently disposable to be sacrificed on gears of power. All this accumulation of deeds has irrevocably shaped the ørlog of the world and everything living in it, imprinting collective trauma deep into wyrd.

Nothing better affirms this loss of wonder than some of the ways people have sought escape from the endless grind. The thirst for something greater has always strained against the limits imposed by a society with little room for anything spiritual or otherworldly that doesn't fit in preapproved, safely defined boxes. Popular culture since the late 1990s has seen a consistent stream of stories injecting a bit of magic into life. Everything from the sprawling urban fantasy genre, where werewolves and vampires stalk urban nights, fae dwell just around the corner, and fantastical feats of spellwork are possible, to magical realist tales depicting a world where the mundane hums with life, animation, and agency. Similar escapes are also found in musical subcultures ranging from the macabre beauty of all things gothic to the pounding, epic fury of heavy metal and the visceral ecstasy of the growing neofolk scene where participants cocreate new forms of personal expression infused with a greater sense of wonder and potential.

The answer to the problem of disenchantment is embracing reenchantment. This is a process of finding ways to insert more wonder, possibility, and mystery in how you live. It calls for reassessing how we view the world, interact with our environments, and repair the relationships sundered by centuries of historical trauma. As Beckett argues, "The foundation for enchantment begins with recognizing the inherent value and worth of every person, every creature, every ecosystem, every thing."[7] This is possible because our capacity to see the world in such an expansive fashion never left us, even though it has been brutally suppressed. Initiating this healing of our enchantment with the world depends on changing how we interact with everything in it. Reenchantment represents more than adhering to some sort of revived superstition or ritualistic play-acting. It calls for a total shift in our core assumptions about what is and is not valued in the world. It represents a direct challenge to many of the central assumptions guiding modern society.

---

7. Beckett, "4 Steps to Re-enchant the World."

Heath proposes for going even further, arguing for what she describes as a restoration of the relationships that have been sundered by these centuries of destruction. She asserts the emphasis on shifting perspective is insufficient to truly address the sheer scope of the harm done. Instead, she proposes going beyond reenchantment through a process of restoration that focuses on making amends for the harms done during the process of disenchantment, commodification, and imperialism. To put it in more directly Heathen terms, restoration is a recognition of great weregild that is owed and must be paid through repairing the damage done by these violent processes.[8]

From a Radical perspective, reenchantment and restoration are necessary for developing modern Heathen practice and flow logically from the core ideas, assumptions, and arguments presented. Reenchantment engages with the deep anxieties and uncertainties inflicted by modern life, offering a framework for unraveling these designs and opening your perspectives to new possibilities. This can be done, as argued by Beckett and Heath, by engaging in practices that affirm a new, more respectful relationship with the natural world including pilgrimages, wandering in natural spaces, and building relationships with the Powers who are the closest to your daily life. Restoration, in concurrence with Heath's argument, then follows as a necessary next step that all practitioners must take, which includes everything from supporting new nature sanctuaries to honoring these long-denied, often abused Powers. Shifting your perspectives and values from accepting the disenchantment implicit in capitalist realism to a reenchanted worldview opens the way for building these ties with the world around you and repairing the countless seasons of damage done.[9]

This is not to say that reenchantment suggests you can rewrite your own reality at will and without regard for the consent or existence of others. Reenchanting, regardless of method, hinges heavily on becoming more engaged with reality rather than less. Many unexpected insights, ecstasy, and flashes of penetrating understanding flow from shifting your perspectives outside of the ordinary. A good way to think of reenchantment is it encourages you to change your position and look at everything from a different angle. It is not some kind of promise of fantastical, secret powers over material existence.

---

8. Heath, "Restoration, Not Reenchantment."

9. Heath, "Restoration, Not Reenchantment."

Leaving behind such notions of power over and through hidden knowledge is also essential for conducting a more thorough restoration process. As Cat Heath argues, the disenchantment of the world in the Americas was a direct extension of the colonial drive of conquest blazing from 1492 on, which offered no room for anything that did not fit in their prescribed world order. Implicit in this genocidal impulse is a desire to assert dominion and rule over the land, bending natural forces to the demands of the new order with little regard for the potential harm this brought.[10] This, therefore, argues for approaching any relationships with the Powers or the Otherworlds from a place of humility, cooperation, and respect instead of aspiring to rule and command. Restoration, from a Radical perspective, depends on rebuilding and replacing the assumptions, arguments, and institutions responsible for disenchantment, colonization, empire, and enclosure with more just, equitable, and genuinely representative alternatives, practices, and solutions.

rite
INVOKING FIRE AND ICE

One rite that taps directly into changing and shifting this relationship is Invoking Fire and Ice. This rite is widely used in Fire and Ice practice for preparing a space for further rites, rituals, and trancework. This example of the rite is a simple, stripped-down version that can be made as elaborate or kept as simple as you feel is necessary. What is important is invoking the opposing forces of fire and ice in a way that leads to them meeting, joining, and creating a new synthesis of possibility and space for new creation.

rite

Stand or sit in front of your altar facing toward it. Perform the Understanding the Breath exercise listed in appendix I.

Open both of your hands with your palms facing upward. Slowly chant the word *Isaz*, the name of the Elder Futhark rune of ice. As you chant, visualize the rune, which is shown below, being drawn on the palm of your dominant hand.

---

10. Heath, "Restoration, Not Reenchantment."

I

Feel the power of ice fill that hand.

Slowly chant the word *Kenaz*, the name of the Elder Futhark rune of the torch and fire. As you chant, visualize the rune Kenaz, as shown below, being drawn on the palm of your nondominant hand.

Feel the power of fire fill that hand and sit with the opposing forces for a moment.

Clap your hands together while breathing in and pull them apart slowly as you breathe out, with both palms facing each other for a moment. Feel the energy of the moment of creation, a reflection of the time when the fire of Muspelheim and the ice of Niflheim met in the Ginnungagap.

Turn both hands away from each other, palms open, and face them toward the altar. Keep your palms open and facing out as you slowly sweep your extended arms until they are pointing in opposite directions, one on each side of your body held up at shoulder height.

Stay in place, holding your arms out, while turning one full circle. As you sweep your arms, feel the energy of the moment spread around you and push outward in every direction, opening the space for new possibilities.

Beyond Coincidence

If reenchantment represents a shift in how you understand your relationships with the world around you, synchronicity is best understood as one of the more common features of this shift of perspective and the shifts in consciousness brought on by the ecstatic state. It is, paraphrasing witch author and blogger Mat Auryn, a tendency to notice unexpected moments in life best described as omens, signs, and unlikely coincidences.[11] What makes such instances synchronicity is if they happen to coincide with ritual work, divination, or taking of omens in ways that seem inexplicable in the moment.

There are many different ways synchronicity manifests for practitioners from small and subtle to loud and epic. Examples include a rumble of thunder interrupting ritual, a raven's feather falling from the sky during a trance session, multiple sets of paired objects breaking during the course of an ecstatic performance celebrating the god Loki, unexpected flashes of insight after seeing something you associate with a specific Power, and more. Each event, on its own, was the result of very clear, discrete causes that can be materially measured, such as cups being banged too hard on tables, atmospheric conditions, and ravens shedding feathers in flight.

What makes the specific occurrences synchronicity is that these moments happened in a time, place, and fashion that already carried a specific spiritual significance, such as ritual, meditation, and epiphany. It is the unlikelihood of the specific coincidences of unexpected thunder during ritual or raven feathers after trance, both of which have deep associations with specific gods, which makes these instances synchronicity. Such unexpected moments are often interpreted by practitioners as carrying rich, potential meaning, though the specifics will greatly vary from case to case and person to person.

When you accept synchronicity into your life, you should refrain as much as possible from actively imposing meaning where it might not be present. Not all moments of coincidence are necessarily instances of synchronicity. Sometimes a flock of ravens chattering on the power line is just a conspiracy of ravens and not a visit from the god of victory to remind you that your utility bill is overdue or that a blackout is imminent. The most significant instances of synchronicity

---

11. Mat Auryn, "Synchronicity and the Psychic Witch," Patheos Pagan, June 26, 2017, https://www.patheos.com/blogs/matauryn/2017/06/26/synchronicity-witch/.

are those that happen during or in close relationship to a trance session, ritual, or ecstatic states when perceptions are altered, making practitioners most open to otherworldly insights. This is not to say such conditions are necessary, however, for a moment of meaningful coincidence to be synchronicity. Otherwise, it is very easy to impose a cycle of self-reinforcing, ego-bloating reflection that leaves you bereft of the means to perceive what is genuinely happening in the world around you.

Cultivating discernment around synchronicity requires developing a very multifaceted understanding of the world around you. Synchronicities are far from the only source of information present in the modern world for practitioners that are worth considering when making major decisions or confronting serious dilemmas. These moments should be treated as one more datapoint to consider or perspective to examine rather than the most significant or central source of information. Just because a Power may have an opinion on how you should approach a problem or conflict does not mean that perspective is necessarily the best course of action given your circumstances. You are neither required to accept one specific interpretation of a synchronicity event nor expected to proceed based solely on this moment of synchronicity. Sometimes there may be moments where such a meaningful coincidence urges you toward a specific course of action, and there is nothing wrong with this. What is important is to take in this information in conjunction with all other relevant, significant factors before acting, whether the synchronicity is an early occurrence that sets a chain of events in motion or manifests at what feels to be a critical moment of decision.

The sense of communion associated with synchronicity is a direct reflection of the deep, fundamental connections within Nordic cosmology between beings, worlds, and wyrd. For Fire and Ice practice, there is no inherent separation between us, the Powers, their realms, and the greater forces that bind together the cosmos. This immanence is part of living in a world where everything around us must be treated with respect, dignity, and affirmation of its existence, as there are no hard-and-fast boundaries between us and the Powers.

This acceptance of deep, mutual interconnectivity is what Dr. Rune Rasmussen, founder and host of the Nordic Animism YouTube channel, calls continuous cosmology. This refers to metaphysical systems that view the barriers between human and the otherworldly as more porous and connected. As he described it in a personal interview with me, the human and otherworldly "are tightly bound together. Often there's a bond by which the tree is holding the serpents in creating the ordered world.... The other is bounded to the foundational principle of the lifeworld in the Ockelbo stone."

The Ockelbo stone was a Swedish runestone that was found in 1795 in a church's foundation and was removed, stored, and sketched by local artists. The original was destroyed in a fire in 1904, and it was reconstructed in 1932 based on these surviving sketches.[12] Rasmussen described it as a map of reality for the pre-Christian Nordic peoples, calling attention to details such as a tree that seems to be growing a dragon or a serpent. The tree represented organic living and a friendly world in very tight relation with chaos, the serpent.

He further explained in our conversation that there are two important human figures. One seems to be approaching the tree holding a horn, almost as if offering a libation to the tree. The other figure is holding the tree with one hand and in the other hand a ring, the symbol of both swearing and creating connection. The tree in this continuous cosmology symbolizes both the dynamic exchange and unity between the ordered part of reality and the threat to the order of product reality or the ego.

As Rasmussen further argued in our interview, this stands in stark contrast with the broader assumptions that guide a modern, Christian-influenced capitalist society that depends on much starker divisions between humanity and the divine. In Christianity, for instance, the really important distinction is between interior humanity and exterior reality, the distinction between humanity and God. In polytheist religions, such as the Afro-Brazilian religion Candomble, marriage between God and humanity is the biggest and most important purpose of the religion all the way through. Rasmussen is absolutely convinced the pre-Christian Nordic religion also had the polytheist view.

Continuous cosmology is the capstone of a broader understanding of reality and spirituality. It is part of a worldview that emphasizes connection and relationship over separation and dualistic thinking that flows naturally from the surviving source material. For modern Heathens, the Powers and Otherworlds are not untouchable by mortals but are just as much a part of our daily lives as anything else.

---

12. Viking Archeology, "Ockelbo Runestone," accessed June 13, 2022, http://viking
    .archeurope.info/index.php?page=ockelbo-runestone.

exercise

THREE GROUNDING BREATHS

The Three Grounding Breaths is an exercise used to safely conclude an extended trance state. You should do the Three Grounding Breaths at the conclusion of any trancework to help bring yourself back into the physical world. This exercise can also be used to quickly bring a practitioner out of an ecstatic state of consciousness. Pulling this proverbial emergency brake is not encouraged and should only be done if you feel endangered or are suffering serious psychological harm from your experiences in trance. If this is ever necessary, please give yourself the time for extended aftercare and recovery, as an emergency transition from an altered state can be very disorienting.

Begin by breathing in swiftly through your nose, feeling the breath travel down through your body to the ends of your fingers and the tips of your toes.

Breathe out swiftly from your mouth, feeling the rush of air as it leaves your body and empties your lungs.

Breathe in again through your nose, feeling the breath tickle the ends of your ears, the back of your neck, and the tip of your nose.

Breathe out swiftly from your mouth, expelling all the air in your lungs in a measured, rapid fashion.

Breathe in one more time through your nose, feeling the breath fill you steadily as you open your eyes and take in the world around you.

Breathe out steadily through your mouth as you take in your surroundings with all your senses.

chapter two
WYRD

Boldness is better than plaints can be
For those whose feet must fare;
To a destined day has mine age been doomed,
And my life's span thereto laid.
—Skirnismol 13, *Poetic Edda*

If all of reality could be described as an endless song, then wyrd is the tempo setting the rhythm of existence. *Wyrd* is often translated as the Old Nordic word for "fate," yet there is so much more to this beautiful system of understanding. Wyrd shapes the experiences, history, and potential facing all things in all worlds. In doing so, it binds all realms together in an endless dance of creation, change, life, and death. Shaped in part by the Norns, wyrd is one of the only constants in Nordic practice that is essential for understanding how individuals and groups exercise agency.

In modern society, fate usually has dour implications. However, Nordic wyrd is best understood as a metaphysical force comparable to gravity or magnetism that operates in consistent patterns that are shaped by the two essential forces of ørlog and hamingja. This stands in contrast to other models, such as the random unpredictability of the Wheel of Fortune or the whims of an all-powerful, inescapable, and conscious governing force such as you may see with the Christian concept of the will of God. Wyrd is an endlessly emergent, self-perpetuating, and organically shaped process with no single will but is the result of the actions of all beings of every world. This is illustrated in a symbol known as the Web of Wyrd:

Figure 2. Web of Wyrd

The two core forces driving wyrd are ørlog and hamingja. Ørlog consists of all the existing circumstances confronting all beings in the Nine Worlds.[13] It includes everything from your present social and material conditions to inalterable facts regarding your life, such as where, when, and to whom you are born and everything connected to those conditions.

Hamingja represents each being's capacity to cause change to existing ørlog. Hamingja is further broken into two subcomponents: gipta, which refers to what you are given by your origins, and gæfu, which refers to your personal abilities and skills.[14] Combined, they make your personal hamingja, which can be changed by later actions or alterations to existing ørlog. In Fire and Ice practice, hamingja can even be pooled for collective efforts, creating a far greater force for change than any one participant could harness on their own.

Actions, their consequences, and how they change your existing conditions alters and, in some cases, can help create new ørlog, reshaping the parameters of existence. How significant this change is depends on what ørlog is altered

---

13. Patricia M. Lafayllve, *A Practical Heathen's Guide to Asatru* (Woodbury, MN: Llewellyn Publications, 2013), 102–5; Cat Heath, *Elves, Witches & Gods: Spinning Old Heathen Magic in the Modern Day* (Woodbury, MN: Llewellyn Publications, 2021), 100–6.

14. Mathias Nordvig, *Ásatrú for Beginners: A Modern Heathen's Guide to the Ancient Northern Way* (Emeryville, CA: Rockridge Press, 2020), 26–27.

and how this happens, all of which is made possible through beings using their hamingja to create changes in existence. Some ørlog, such as that which is related to one specific person's conditions, is easier to change than the ørlog of powerful institutions that are sustained by the deliberate actions of multiple beings.

Studying these interactions reveals wyrd is an unceasing dynamic driving all of reality with constant motion. This continuous process has no specific starting point or end goal. Practically speaking, this means no one is burdened with the weight of a special purpose or role. Your destiny is defined by you, what you face, and how you respond to the world around you and not by the demands of inscrutable deities or karmic debt. You may not get to choose the time you come into the world, but you can decide what you will do about it. Your actions can also change the world for the better in ways great and small, some of which may blossom long after you pass on. The logic of wyrd lays bare that every action and every choice matters, giving practitioners tremendous spiritual freedom to define themselves on their terms.

Under the metaphysical framework of wyrd, there are beginnings and endings, but there is no one specific beginning or specific ending. Even the final battle of Ragnarök is, itself, only final for this present iteration of reality, as is suggested by the promise of a new, green world that comes after Surtr's firestorm dies down and is shaped by the actions of the preceding epoch. On a more individual level, births and deaths are beginnings and endings for that aspect of a person's existence. Their influence does not cease with the end of physical existence but continues through the ørlog that resulted from each person's deeds and through their new form of existence that results from the process of dying.

Wyrd, in short, places the emphasis on what your actions mean in the here and now and what consequences flow from them. Your main responsibility under wyrd is considering the ramifications of your deeds and how they will shape the world around you. Even death, which brings a final reward or punishment in many Christian denominations, does not absolve a person of their duty to craft worthy ørlog, lend their hamingja to good causes, and give their best to the wyrd around them. Such choices will echo long after your bones have become dust and all recollection of your deeds are lost. Even in this moment the actions of those nameless, forgotten people in history continue to shape wyrd simply by virtue of the way their struggles shaped the world of the present day.

These core concepts of wyrd are just the beginning of understanding how this central, essential force shapes life in Nordic Pagan practice. Everything in the Nine Worlds is subject to wyrd, and understanding wyrd on a deeper level helps you navigate your experiences and helps explain how the broader patterns of reality take shape. This, naturally, brings the conversation to the Norns, the beings who are often seen as central to these processes, and how wyrd as a vast, seemingly unconscious force can be squared with the animate, deliberate actions of these beings. Answering this dilemma requires a deeper exploration of who the Norns are, what they represent, and how these entities influence these patterns.

The Norns

The Powers who are most associated with wyrd itself are the Norns. They are a vast collective of related beings consisting of two main groups: the Three Greater Norns (known as Urdr, Verðandi, and Skuld) and the many lesser Norns, who follow all beings.

All Norns are described in surviving source material as having a very direct, powerful relationship with wyrd and how it takes shape. The Three, as will be discussed further, are instrumental to the development of the broader patterns of wyrd, while the lesser Norns associated with particular people or wyrds are described as responsible for deciding their fortunes. The existence of the Norns raises serious questions on how you could describe wyrd as an organic, constantly emergent process when there are Powers who have direct influence over said process. The answer lies in understanding more about the Norns, what they represent, and how they interact with wyrd.[15]

Of the Norns, the Three are the most well-known and are responsible for shaping the wyrd of the Nine Worlds. They are at least as old as Midgard, as shown in their first appearance in the Voluspo:

---

15. Karen Bek-Pedersen, *The Norns in Old Norse Mythology* (Edinburgh, UK: Dunedin Academic Press, 2011), 13–14.

> In their dwellings at peace they played at tables,
> Of gold no lack did the gods then know,—
> Till thither came up giant-maids three,
> Huge of might, out of Jotunheim.[16]

According to Snorri Sturluson, they dwell in the Hall of Urðarbrunnr by the roots of Yggdrasil. He describes Urdr, Verðandi, and Skuld drawing sand and water from the Well of Urdr that is used to help keep the World Tree nourished. In the Voluspo, their work is described much more directly than Sturluson's metaphorical description:

> Thence come the maidens mighty in wisdom,
> Three from the dwelling down 'neath the tree;
> Urth is one named, Verthandi the next,—
> On the wood they scored,—and Skuld the third.
> Laws they made there, and life allotted
> To the sons of men, and set their fates.[17]

Through this labor, they sustain Yggdrasil and keep it growing despite Nidhoggr's endless gnawing below. As they work, they steadily shape the World Tree's wyrd and, through Yggdrasil's connections to all of existence, define the wyrd of all Nine Worlds.[18]

As central as the Greater Norns are in Nordic cosmology, there is a surprising lack of any direct interest shown by them. No surviving source ever describes them as showing interest in any person, group, or place's existence or lack thereof. There are no suggestions that specific grains of wood, drafts of water, or handfuls of sand represent any particular person, place, thing, or Power. All sources largely agree the Three's most immediate concern is doing what they can to help Yggdrasil thrive. The Three carry out their work without any particular judgment or agenda, as their labors are necessary to keep

---

16. Henry Adams Bellows, trans., *The Poetic Edda: The Mythological Poems* (Mineola, NY: Dover Publications, 2004), Voluspo 8.
17. Bellows, *The Poetic Edda*, Voluspo 20.
18. Snorri Sturluson, *The Prose Edda: Norse Mythology*, trans. and ed. Jesse L. Byock (New York: Penguin Books, 2005), Gylfaginning 15.

everything moving. They are facilitators, caregivers, and midwives to renewed possibility for all the cosmos whose main priority is perpetuating the greater cycle.

More of why the Three seem separated from the processes of reality is seen in the meanings of their names. *Urdr* is the Old Norse word for both "was," often understood as the past, and "fate," representing all that has happened in the past leading up to this moment. *Verðandi*, also from Old Norse, translates to "existence" and "what is becoming," an understanding of the present moment that emphasizes its place as a place of decision instead of simply as a space in time. *Skuld* is the Old Norse word for both "debt," in the form of what is owed as a consequence of actions taken and harms done, and "shall be," suggesting what future will emerge as a direct consequence of what was and is becoming.[19]

These names directly tie the Three to the passage of events on the most fundamental level, directly connecting them to the march of the seasons, the movements of the sun and moon, and the rhythms of the tides. They are some of the most primordial of all the Powers, responsible for functions that shape everything in all forms of existence. Even their core nature is hotly debated in academic circles. According to scholar Karen Bek-Pedersen, there is considerable argument about whether these Norns are a three-in-one figure, three distinct beings, or even potentially manifestations of the greater whole of the Norns with the Three serving as avatars of specific aspects of their greater collective.[20]

This association may provide an explanation for why the Three are described as having no close relationship with any specific consequence of their tending of the World Tree. Being fundamentally tied to the pulse that drives all of existence, bringing equal measures of age and entropy with change and new vitality, places the Three Norns in a deeply primal, removed place far beyond the machinations of others. If you see the Three as manifestations of the whole of the Norns, then this would further distance them from being god-like beings shaping existence and more strongly emphasize their role as facilitators of existence. What they do is both incredibly intimate yet totally removed from any particular wyrd, shaping

---

19. Bek-Pedersen, *The Norns in Old Norse Mythology*, 77.

20. Bek-Pedersen, *The Norns in Old Norse Mythology*, 78–81.

the possibilities of all things from a great distance with little attachment to any particular outcome beyond maintaining the cycle.

Such detachment is further reinforced by how endless work is also done in total isolation from the other Powers and worlds. There are no examples of any Powers directly approaching the Three by the well or any mention of journey to their hall. There is also scant evidence of the Nordic peoples worshiping or directly interacting with them. Their influence is unquestionable, yet they remain aloof from the Nine Worlds even as they shape the contours of existence for all beings. This suggests what the Three do, how they carry it out, and what it means for the world is fundamentally incomprehensible or at least sufficiently intimidating to deter prying eyes. You could infer the Norns are free to act as they will, carrying out whatever inscrutable agenda moves them. This, however, seems unlikely for the Three, as there is no mention or implication in surviving source material of them being involved in the affairs of any other being or Power.

Their work sets them apart in such a fundamental way that they have no apparent concern for anything beyond continuing their vocation. Such a lack of evidence of any real goals or agenda shows them as the framers of wyrd in a deeply profound way, which, ultimately, is still shaped by how they interact with other forces in the Nine Worlds much like everything else interacts with wyrd. Even as the Three are often depicted as the closest possible embodiment of fate and destiny in Nordic practice, they are still interacting with wyrd and its forces in a very similar way to everything else.

The Three are not alone in this work. Lesser Norns are scattered throughout the Nine Worlds, collectively doing their labor of giving form to wyrd as it moves and takes shape. They move invisibly, assigning both good and bad fortune to people for their own inscrutable reasons. Many characters in the sagas have lamented the ill will of these Norns, cursing them for placing them in such impossible circumstances. Though this lends the impression of the Norns as ineffable architects of wyrd, there is the possibility they were still subject to wyrd in their own ways.[21]

One excellent example of this possibility is the evocative expression "to make the Norns weep." This phrase is often used in the sagas as a reference to

---

21. Bek-Pedersen, *The Norns in Old Norse Mythology*, 23.

scenes of awful violence, carrying the implication of Norns lamenting the horrors they were still somehow compelled to further shape.

One element regarding these Norns is how their judgments are referred to in a legalistic sense, giving further weight to the significance of the tendency for them to appear in collective groups. Nordic justice was done by a collective court of the community where Thing assemblies passed laws and settled disputes, making law and its enforcement a very communal process. It, therefore, makes a certain sense for cosmic decisions to be handled in a similar fashion. These animistic Powers are collectively responsible for giving shape to wyrd, making them partially culpable for how events play out even while they are still at the mercy of greater forces in wyrd.[22]

Just as there is little to no evidence of the Urdr, Verðandi, and Skuld receiving evidence or petitions of aid, the same is true of the lesser Norns. Totally absent are any charms or incantations meant to win the favor of these mysterious entities, a state which is compounded by the utter lack of any traditions similar to leaving offerings for house and land spirits, which are a constant in other aspects of Nordic animism. Nothing comparable to the rampant evidence of other animistic or votive practices dedicated to other Powers is present, strongly suggesting the lesser Norns were just as unapproachable as the Three.[23]

A modern practitioner could interpret the work of the lesser Norns as the facilitators of acts of random chance. You could see their capricious, unknowable choices for the immediate moment as something like fortune or what the modern world describes as luck. They can be found in the flip of a coin, the roll of a dice, or any other seemingly random and causeless development. This places them in a pervasive, intimate role in the Nordic cosmos. The lesser Norns' constant, invisible work ensures these small moments happen, forcing critical changes to ørlog and in turn the unfolding of wyrd. They live at the intersections of ørlog and hamingja that make wyrd what it is, putting them at the crossroads of every possibility.

How they work is unclear, though it is possible that one could infer the processes are similar to another wyrd-laden group of Powers in the Nine Worlds. Valkyries, the ferocious war spirits who quite literally choose the slain with the

---

22. Bek-Pedersen, *The Norns in Old Norse Mythology*, 23–26, 33.

23. Bek-Pedersen, *The Norns in Old Norse Mythology*, 32–33.

trajectory of every arrow and the swing of every sword on every battlefield, are beings who are very closely connected with wyrd. Their place in shaping the outcomes of conflict makes their work somewhat like that of the lesser Norns, a role that is further emphasized in Sturluson's work, which claims the Norn Skuld is also a Valkyrie who stalks the battlefields of the world. There is no implication in the surviving source material that Valkyries were physically in-carnate in the conflicts where they chose who would be slain in direct, visceral ways, yet their influence over war was indisputable.[24]

It is therefore reasonable to infer these lesser Norns, collectively, have an enormous amount of power over wyrd. This could, therefore, suggest that if the Norns were to act in an organized fashion, then they would have un-assailable sway over existence, making them the authors of all destinies. This possibility is, however, simply not present anywhere in the lore. Nowhere is it suggested the Norns act in a collective, organized fashion or work to im-plement some sort of predetermined agenda. They, like the Three Tenders of Yggdrasil, simply do as they will with little apparent input from other Powers, Norns, or other entities scattered throughout the Nine Realms. This status as facilitators and at times complicators of wyrd is bounded by many of the same patterns influencing all other beings in existence.

Such an arrangement of beings ranging from the drivers of time to the shapers of each being's fortunes shows a deeply animistic understanding of re-ality. This situation reinforces the central dynamics of wyrd as consistent, per-vasive, and present through all of existence. It is, after all, only fitting that a metaphysical constant that is the product of actions is itself driven by constant action. Such consistency in wyrd's core patterns reinforces how genuinely fun-damental they are to existence. Yet even as their actions directly and indirectly impact everyone's lives, they are still ultimately additional elements shaping a broader framework. They cannot and do not override the autonomy of any being even as their actions may present vexing barriers or unexpected windfalls for their goals. What you do about these challenges is still up to you. Even if the Norns may seem to be totally against you, it is still possible to challenge such misfortune and actively shape your wyrd.

---

24. Bek-Pedersen, *The Norns in Old Norse Mythology*, 54–56.

They also, in their isolation and separation from the affairs of the world around them, effectively personify those things that are beyond your seeming control yet have pervasive influence over your life. The Three Tenders, as representatives of time's inexorable march, bring with them the influence of constant, unending changes that everyone must negotiate throughout their time in Midgard. The lesser Norns, similarly, stand in beautifully for those little events, sometimes frustrating and other times celebrated, which directly shape how the world unfolds around you.

The question the Norns, greater and lesser, then pose is how will you respond to these forces that stand beyond your grasp? That such things exist is indisputable. Everyone, from the greatest of Gods and the World Tree itself to the smallest of things in the Nine Worlds, is still subject to things that lie beyond control and sometimes even beyond understanding. Wyrd and the Norns remind us to consider these potentialities while also accepting our lack of direct agency over how they will manifest.

That the Norns exist more as shapers and facilitators of wyrd than authors of its design reinforces this truth. The uncertainties and harsh realities they embody are real, without any doubt. Such existence does not imply, however, that any specific end is any more foreordained than any other. Wyrd, with the help of the Norns, is always in motion, and the space for carving out new possibility is always present, no matter how small or distant it may become. No matter how dire conditions may become, the best response is to seize the moment and take charge of how your wyrd will take shape. Such capacity exists within all beings and is the essence of what makes wyrd, as facilitated by the labor of the Norns, possible.

Such defying of the inescapable can take on many forms, great and small. Not every instance of delaying or thwarting the inevitable takes the shape of a cosmic battle or cruel execution, but regardless of the form it takes, the core of the response is always one of creating new possibility. Just as the Norns must endlessly labor to sustain life, so too does every being struggle to fulfill their wyrd as fully and on their own terms as they possibly can.

Living a Wyrding Way

For some, the kind of all-encompassing influence of wyrd and its Norn tenders presents intimidating challenges to how one might understand life. Its sheer immensity and pervasive reach can make wyrd into a truly intimidating force, giving the impression that our lives are detritus floating in a vast ocean stirred by the movements of incomprehensibly vast, utterly inhuman tides. Such a reaction is perfectly understandable, especially given many of the default assumptions that come with the modern world's highly atomized understanding of the individual, in which identity is heavily mediated through consumer choices.

To anyone who is raised in an environment where one's being is limited solely to the edges of their form and not much beyond, suggesting that life is part of a vast, complex dance with the totality of creation can feel very diminishing. For those who are used to a more modern Christian understanding of enforced binaries in which one's personal relationship with God bypasses all other concerns, learning of wyrd may feel as though you are subjecting yourself to an even more alien, incomprehensible set of dictates without even a promise of divine reward or threat of eternal punishment. In practice, wyrd is neither of these possibilities and offers potential avenues for liberation from the philosophical shackles that come with both sets of perspectives.

On the question of individual agency, wyrd makes it clear each person has more power over their life and the world around them than either the atomized individual or the obedient follower of God's plan. Under wyrd, the simple truth that our lives are the sum of our experiences, the conditions that shaped them, and our capacity to respond to such developments is an affirmation of what some might describe as a genuinely materialist understanding of the world. Recognizing these influences and the role they play in shaping each individual's wyrd is the first step to being able to truly take charge of how you respond to such conditions. To limit one's focus, as entirely too many in the commodified, consumer world of today do, if unintentionally, to solely your own immediate capacity in the most mundane sense can limit your view of greater possibilities. Wyrd's mechanisms depend on connection and relationship. Understanding these factors in your life can open up new perspectives on both how a particular problem may have emerged and how you can also solve it.

This is especially true of institutional or societal problems, both of which a highly individualistic, consumerist mentality is woefully unequipped to handle. For those who live according to a narrowly atomized view, regardless of if they call themselves liberals or conservatives, everything is purely the product of individual choices and prejudices. Even the influence of greater institutions is, ultimately, a matter of individual preferences and choices in spite of ample evidence that existing social systems exercise considerable sway over both. Individuals still have choices, after all, even though such choices are heavily constrained by circumstances.

It is here that a wyrd-influenced frame of understanding creates new possibilities for addressing this problem that modern, atomized individualism cannot. Under wyrd, our present social and ecological crises' institutional, societal, and collectively driven roots are the clear product of centuries' worth of ørlog accumulated by countless actors. These decisions changed the circumstances facing those who followed after them while carving out a path of least resistance, which, unbeknownst to them but abundantly clear today, became an increasingly steep slide into oblivion. Wyrd's wisdom does not diminish the scale of the challenge ahead—far from it. What it does is answer the question of what is to be done with deliberate, sustained, organized effort to consciously transform the ørlog driving our conditions into a new, more truly sustainable ørlog.

How this is done is explained by hamingja, each person's luck and ability to change the world around them. Hamingja already demonstrates that, within wyrd, everything already has at least some means on its own to influence the ørlog they interact with, including the ørlog passed down from what was.

Where hamingja particularly emphasizes capacity to cause change is in how it is frequently described as being transferable. The sagas have multiple examples of people extending their hamingja to others, particularly those who are preparing to engage in battle, to lend them strength, courage, and other kinds of support. This metaphysical form of collective action is further reinforced by examples of the Powers working collectively to achieve greater ends, such as the slaying of Ymir by Odin, Vili, and Ve and the creation of Midgard by all the gods. Such an understanding of wyrd leaves it clear that any ørlog that is too great for one or a few to alter can be changed or even completely abolished by the concentrated efforts of many endowed with sufficient shared hamingja to accomplish this goal.

Such a struggle will not be quick or easy but, as the example of Odin's slaying of Ymir shows, such a radical change in existence is very possible provided our deeds are done with an eye toward achieving this broader end. Under wyrd, such an approach is not only advisable, but it makes far more sense than claiming that the influence of your actions starts and stops at the shallow, false choices offered by our endlessly marketized society.

This truly begs the question of how wyrd is offering something other than submission to a new kind of divine master who has written your destiny before you were even born. Some might even point to the names of the Three by the Well, particularly Skuld as "shall be," to argue that wyrd is simply another form of predestination with all the lack of agency this implies. Such questions have a grain of truth to them, as much of the discussion of wyrd in the source material carries an air of inevitability. Such descriptions, combined with an almost stoic acceptance of adversity by the characters of the sagas, give wyrd an air of predetermination.

It is at this juncture that Heathen philosophy, based on the example from ancients and the sagas, diverges sharply from the strongly deterministic implications of wyrd. For many modern readers, it may make sense for people to simply accept the dynamics unfolding in the greater design of existence, find ways to push where they can make their circumstances more comfortable, and otherwise go with the flow. This is the exact moment where Heathenry of all stripes argues, instead, for being an active, bold participant in shaping wyrd instead of passively acquiescing to one's fate. Challenges, dangers, and even the seemingly unbeatable were all meant to be confronted even if taking such a course of action would lead to your demise. For Heathens, as the following examples will show, what matters most when facing long or even insurmountable odds is that you actively shape your wyrd through your deeds based on sources both mythic and historic.

From a mythic standpoint, nothing better illustrates this idea of facing one's destiny and taking active steps to shape it than the certainty of Ragnarök. Though it is certainly debatable when and how the contents of the Voluspo became common knowledge for the Powers, there does not seem to be any evidence in surviving lore suggesting it was anything less than an accepted fact. The Aesir know, through this vision, that they will face a very grim, bloody battle that will consume most of their lives and the Nine Worlds with them. Odin and Thor are specifically prophesied to be devoured whole by Fenrir and overcome by the venom of the Midgard Serpent. It cannot be overstated how absolutely clearly the Voluspo paints this picture; not only do the gods know they will lose, but they've already been given blow-by-blow accounts of how it will all happen eons before the battle will occur. This absolute certainty is what makes their preparations for battle even more impressive, showing even in the face of ultimate defeat the gods will still actively define how their doom unfolds.[25]

A similar defiant streak runs amok through surviving historical sources. Tales abound in available materials of famous Viking warriors almost eagerly defying the possibility of death on a regular basis and even expressing surprising resistance in the face of the unavoidable. Of all these, the purported fate of Ragnar Lodbrok probably best summarizes this ideal of unceasing resistance when the famed Viking raider faced his death in King Aella's snake pit. Seeing no hope of escape, Ragnar instead faced his death with a certain kind of grim humor. One of the two surviving versions of this saga claims his last words were "Oh how the piglets will squeal when they hear how the old boar died!" alluding to his faith that his sons would avenge his death, while the other, more ominously, simply records Ragnar laughing maniacally in the face of his enemies as the poison and serpents overcame him.[26] Regardless of which version you prefer, both show the hero actively defying his foes by either promising they would suffer a terrible vengeance or making a mockery of the whole affair. Even though Ragnar Lodbrok died in that snake pit, how he is said to have faced it reverberates long after his demise by the simple virtue of that he actively defined it according to his terms.

This expectation of defiance, therefore, suggests both that wyrd was something that could be changed by our actions and that those changes happen in a discernible fashion rather than simply manifesting due to the capricious whims of ineffable cosmic forces. There is some truth to this view, though deeper reflection reveals there is much more at work in wyrd than simple, predetermined outcomes or random causality. In wyrd, everything that exists is directly shaped by the ørlog, which defines their circumstances and how they use their hamingja to change those conditions. Therefore, everything that exists is a direct product of prior actions of some kind or another and argues all occurrences are the clear, logical consequence of these responses through hamingja

25. Bellows, *Poetic Edda*, Voluspo 53, 56.

26. Thomas Shippey, *Laughing Shall I Die: Lives and Deaths of the Great Vikings* (London: Reaktion Books, 2018), 34–36.

to ørlog. This means everything was, on some level, meant to happen the way it did because of the conditions that led to every specific development. Specific outcomes do not need to be intended or planned for the consequences of actions to have a direct impact on other people, society, or your environment. In this way, everything was meant to happen as an observable, identifiable consequence of previous actions and their impacts on the world.

Ragnarök, when viewed from this perspective, is therefore not an example of predestination but rather the same, underlying logic that applies to everything in existence. Ragnarök's coming is inevitable in much the same way as the march of the seasons, the movement of the tides, and the cycles of life and death. That the Aesir will, someday, face their many foes in battle and be overwhelmed by them is certain, with even some of the details laid out in excruciating detail. This does not, however, fix its occurrence at a specific point in time or in any way diminish the struggles of the gods to delay its coming as much as possible. Though entropy, decay, and death are inevitable, this does not mean they are to be simply submitted to, heeded, or otherwise allowed to unfold unopposed.

rite
SIGRBLÓT, THE BLÓT FOR VICTORY

One rite that speaks most directly to this understanding of wyrd is the sigrblót, the blót (devotional rite) for victory that seeks the favor of the Powers before going into battle. This rite is performed before engaging in a direct, contested struggle with a force, person, or group acting in direct opposition to your goals. It is often invoked by Heathens, particularly in Fire and Ice practice, before engaging in a lengthy task, committing to a broader struggle, or performing a specific, potentially highly risky action. Regardless of how you perform a sigrblót, it can only be used in such moments of oppositional conflict that represent a serious concern for you and your life. Once committed in sigrblót, see it through to whatever end that brings while always seeking to achieve your ultimate goal as best as possible. Though there is no shame in failure, defeat, or setbacks, this does not mean you can use the support the Powers offer toward unjust ends. The Powers do not grant their favor in conflict lightly and frown on any who squander the gifts that come from a sigrblót for dishonorable ends or pursue their goals by employing disgraceful means.

rite

Set sacred space by invoking the powers of Fire and Ice as described in chapter 1.

Ask the vættir of where you will expect to be in struggle for permission to proceed with the rite. It can bring ill-fortune to proceed without the support of the vættir, especially since they will be impacted by your coming conflict. If the place these vættir are associated with is the object of the struggle, then you may include that you wish their permission to stand as their allies. Finish by providing them with an offering after asking for their permission to proceed.

Call on all your ancestors and the ancestors of those present, by lineage, by adoption, and by affinity, to bear witness and lend their strength to the coming struggle. If possible, invoke any ancestors who may have specific interest in this struggle.

Speak the names of the three gods of battle you wish to invoke for this victory blót. Odin, Thor, and Tyr are popular choices thanks to their clear martial associations, but they are not the only gods you could invoke in a sigrblót. Freyja, as Queen of the Valkyries, and Vidar, Odin's avenging son, are also popular options, as are Loki, for confusion and chaos, and Skaði, the Vengeful Hunter. What matters is the three gods you choose have clear associations with struggle and the battle you are facing.

Provide an offering for each of these gods that has been specially prepared for this sigrblót. It can be a disposable material item, such as especially precious food or drink, a poem or song that must only be performed for this specific rite, an object you have created, or whatever else feels like an appropriate offering.

After providing these offerings, call upon specific aspects of the gods invoked by this rite for their aid in the coming days and promise to use whatever they provide in pursuit of victory, whether this struggle is short and swift or lengthy and enduring.

When you have given all the offerings, take a divinatory reading to see what guidance the Powers have to offer you in the coming fight. This can be using whatever methods you feel most comfortable with, such as rune casting and utiseta seiðr. Consider the meanings and potential warnings offered in the reading.

Thank the Powers for their support and assistance in this blót and reaffirm your promise to follow through in your current struggle.

Figure 3. The Black Star

You can, if you wish, design specific bindrunes, sigils, or other workings to augment your sigrblót. One such example is the Black Star, pictured above, which was first crafted for a sigrblót conducted by the Fire and Ice community in 2020. It is a combination of Tiwaz, the Elder Futhark rune of Tyr and justice, and Hagall, the Younger Futhark rune of the hailstone, and is meant to call down victory over fascist groups, organizing, and movements. It has since been used as part of other antifascist workings and is an example of one method you could incorporate into specific sigrblóts to give it greater strength.

Divination and Wyrd

One especially key aspect in this regard lies in the answers provided by Nordic mysticism of seiðr, runic wisdom, and other esoteric traditions common in modern practice. All these forms of Nordic mysticism are deeply rooted in wyrd, with all aspects of it shaped by this mighty, unending force. Although the many mystical arts of Nordic Paganism cannot offer guaranteed outcomes, these practices further reinforce how much agency the individual Nordic Pagan practitioner has. At their most basic level, they confirm wyrd as a knowable, discernible pattern that in turn reinforces how much agency all beings truly have within this understanding of reality beginning with divination.

Modern Nordic practice, Radical or otherwise, has many different forms of divination. Easily the most well-known of all these tools is rune casting, the art of finding guidance and meaning in the patterns present in the runic alphabets. There are also several forms of divination that can be described as different forms of seiðr, a uniquely Nordic form of folk magical practices that all follow the same general wyrd-shaped logic. Within seiðr one can describe the arts of spae, where a practitioner communes with other Powers and in some cases becomes a vessel for them in a similar fashion to mediumship, and utiseta, sitting out for wisdom, as divinatory practices where the adherent receives guidance through several different forms of ecstatic trance.

Regardless of the method, all Nordic divination operates generally on the core assumption that portions of wyrd's design, whether personal, communal, or global, can be discerned and understood through divinatory readings. Such readings could be described as like a ship's navigator observing the stars, currents, and tides, and using this information to determine their vessel's location. Divination provides a sense of your position and relationship to other factors shaping your wyrd and the wyrd of others. Like navigation, these readings give a sense of where you currently are and are likely to end up if your current course remains unchanged. Divination cannot say, for certain, what will happen, and this is because wyrd is always in motion. However, by providing such bearings, they can give a sense of what to do, watch for, and consider.

This is not the only way that you can understand and incorporate divination into your personal practice. For those who take a more secular and less mystical inclination, divinatory tools are a form of guided self-reflection that can provoke deeper thought and contemplation of your place in the world. There are, naturally, limits on how much or little one can glean from these greater patterns. Some might dismiss such shortcomings as proof that divination is little more than unreliable intuition or baseless superstition. Such a perspective stands starkly at odds with the broader processes of knowledge, exploration, and discovery as they have unfolded throughout the ages. All the material sciences began in places of ignorance, forcing scientists to push these boundaries through investigation and experimentation. Early physicists, as one such example, did not need a definitive answer on the nature of light to make observations and draw conclusions from discernible, measurable phenomena, which led to further discoveries.

The same is true of divination. You do not need to know all the factors influencing how wyrd is shaped to take a reading and investigate the implications of their findings. If a divinatory reading is unclear, inconclusive, or introduces more questions than answers, then this begs the practitioner to seek out further information. Divination is one of many tools for understanding wyrd, and regardless of your opinion of such practices, that they exist and were historically used shows wyrd is a force that can be known and understood to some extent. Those who live under its influence move through the world with open eyes, confident that for all the mysteries and uncertainties in the world, it is still possible to understand and consciously direct your place in it.

This acceptance of divination as a valid tool stands in contrast to the general assumptions that exist in broader society. For those coming from a more conservative Christian background, the Nordic Pagan view on divination draws a stark contrast between the treatment of such practices as the work of the devil or usurping God's will by seeking out knowledge through forbidden means. It is also very different from a more mainstream scoffing of divination as fortune-telling or, even worse, a con job meant to prey on people's vulnerabilities. For the modern adherent, divination is a useful set of tools for contemplation and self-reflection that you may choose to include or leave out of your practice.

One specific form of divination that ties closely to wyrd is using utiseta as a divinatory tool. Sitting out, in its most basic form, is a use of the ecstatic state that gives practitioners space to take in whatever wisdom can be found in the wyrd. This approach is a perfectly valid, solid regular practice that is vital for developing a deeper understanding of this form of seiðr, but it is not the only way to use utiseta for divination. More experienced practitioners can use this art for answering specific questions and resolving particular dilemmas.

A core challenge that comes with using utiseta for divination is maintaining the necessary level of mental restraint to both allow for the patterns in wyrd to present themselves and steer the experience sufficiently to gain some sort of clear guidance. Central to utiseta, as shown in the meditative exercises used in this book and in appendix I, is cultivating an observer mentality in which active thoughts are held back during the ecstatic state. This allows you to better take in the information you are receiving. Practically, this means holding back from imposing meaning, order, causality, or structure on what is unfolding when sitting out and allowing what is present to emerge without intervention.

Maintaining such mental restraint can be very challenging to do when you are seeking answers to a direct, specific question. Bringing in specific concerns can open the way for the conscious mind's existing tendency to seek order, patterns, and causality to present itself during an ecstatic state. Your first impulse may be to suppress these tendencies, but this can lead to more focus being placed on them, resulting in a feedback loop of growing commitment and stress on the ecstatic state. A better approach is to instead respond to the desire for imposing meaning and pursuing expected narratives by assuring your conscious, more logical mind that answers will come when the session is over. This, like the logic behind the Calming the Sea and Sky exercise (found in appendix I), provides an immediate resolution that leaves space free for the ecstatic state to unfold.

Another major challenge, particularly for newer practitioners, is understanding what is experienced while sitting out. Though there is considerable variation in how people experience wyrd and utiseta, one consistent tendency is for everything experienced to work based on dream-like logic. This is true whether you see this as a product of giving your subconscious space to move freely or because of plugging your mind directly into the vast force binding all of existence together. What is experienced during utiseta should be understood as symbolic and metaphorical rather than literal.

This means what is important for interpreting these experiences is the meanings you associate with what you experience. If, for example, you are followed by a pair of ravens throughout the session, it is worth beginning first with what you associate ravens with before then moving outward for mythic associations, such as the connections between Odin and the corvids. These meanings may not always be clear or direct in the moment, and you should take your time in unpacking your experiences. It is also important to be open to new or unexpected developments during utiseta, as there are countless ways wyrd may express itself and manifest during an ecstatic state. Literal interpretations should be taken with a great deal of skepticism, as such incidents are very rare, and even when they do occur, not all may be as it seems.

All that said, the specific actions taken to use utiseta as a divination tool are simple. The crucial step for changing a sitting-out session from a time of contemplation and reception to an active search for answers is having a clear sense of your question before beginning the steps laid out in the Going to the Wells exercise in appendix I. Keep this clear in your mind as you move through each step of this exercise without making it the central focus.

When you arrive at the Well of Urdr with your fylgja beside you, let your question pour into the well and then wait to see what unfolds. Less-experienced practitioners should begin with open-ended questions that you do not have especially strong feelings on, as diving into the specifics of problems for which you have very deep feelings and concerns can be very difficult to sort out and at times be overwhelming for newer seiðworkers.

exercise
READING FRIGGA'S LOOM

This next exercise will help practitioners better understand their relationships to wyrd and deepen their skill with utiseta. It is intended to help the practitioner feel their connections to others and the world around them, allowing them to better understand their broader place in wyrd. This exercise achieves this end by providing you with an effective framework for visualizing these connections, how they influence all enmeshed in them and shape each other through their shared interactions.

This meditation draws on the deep associations between the arts of spinning, seiðr, and Frigga's mastery of both. By reaching through your connections in wyrd to other beings and Powers, you can gain some insight into what lies in her great work and better understand what is becoming or shall be from decisions made in the present.

Begin with a cycle of the Understanding the Breath exercise in appendix I. When you have reached a state of physical calm, complete the Calming the Sea and Sky exercise in appendix I. When the sea is smooth and the sky is clear, move on to the next step.

Focus on the relationship you consider to be most important to you. Visualize the impacts of their actions as direct connections to you, taking on the form of rope, chains, web, or whatever other image feels most natural to you.

Consider how their actions connect to other people, places, ideas, or institutions. Focus now on your connection to these secondary elements and how they impact your life.

Pick the secondary connection you feel most strongly. Focus on what this thing, person, idea, place, or institution is connected to and how it is influenced by those factors.

When you are finished, follow the connections back to you. Reflect on how these connections influence each other and are related.

Take some time to reflect on these connections, what they show you, and how they have changed your understanding of your wyrd and the wyrd of others.

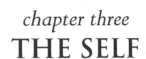

chapter three
THE SELF

An eagle I saw flying from the end through the house,
Our fate must be bad, for with blood he sprinkled us; ...
From the evil I fear that 'twas Atli's spirit.
—Atlamol en Grönlezku 18, *Poetic Edda*

Just as modern Nordic-derived practice views questions of free will, cause and effect, and relationship with the world around us in significantly different ways than modern society, the same is true of how each person is understood. In Radical Nordic Paganism, as inspired by the ancients, the Self is made of four parts known as hamr, your body or physical form; hugr, your consciousness; fylgja, your spiritual shadow; and hamingja, your luck or personal force. Each part of the Self is equally important, with all working together to make up you and every other being in existence.

This four-part self stands in stark contrast with more conventional, modern ideas such as body-mind duality or body-mind-spirit systems. What further complicates this are the significant differences between how these concepts are interpreted in Radical Heathenry and how broadly similar concepts are understood by modern society. Digging deeper into the implications of these divergences and developing more complete relationships with the components of the Self will help you understand your relationship with the world, wyrd, and everything in between. The more you understand these concepts, the better you can change yourself and your circumstances.

The Four-Part Self

Even though each of these four aspects of the modern Heathen Self has its own distinct properties, they all share some key common traits. First and foremost, there is no indication any of these elements is more important than any other. It is through hugr, hamr, hamingja, and fylgja working together that the Self is both possible and fully realized. One does not dictate to the others, as they only effectively come together when they all work in concert. Second, each one is a malleable component, though the ways they can be altered vary. Third, and finally, each of these components is also inextricably connected to the broader world around us while also being shaped by the greater patterns of wyrd. Every being, no matter how great or small, is closely connected to everything else through these relationships that resonate throughout wyrd. These core, consistent elements are important to remember as one considers how the Nordic four-part Self relates with how modern society understands the individual.

Hamr

The best place to start is with the hamr, or your physical form. For many modern people, physical form and body may be seen generally as synonymous concepts, and you may wonder why hamr is not simply known as the body. This is because, based on what is known of the ancients and how this is interpreted in the Way of Fire and Ice, hamr clearly represents more than the limitations of one's flesh, blood, and bone. It was generally understood to represent the whole of how you are perceived and move in the world. According to scholars such as Lyonel Perabo and Neil Price, this term had etymological connections to older words for "skin" or "pelt." Hamr, according to their research, could potentially include one's clothing, personal presentation, demeanor, effects, and even modifications to the body.[27] Hamr, as understood through the surviving sources, is malleable and can be deliberately changed by the hamr's wearer. Neil

---

27. Lyonel D. Perabo, "Shapeshifting in Old Nordic-Icelandic Literature," *Roda da Fortuna: Revista Eletronica sobre Antiguidade e Medievo* 6, no. 1 (2017) 136–37; Neil Price, *The Viking Way: Magic and Mind in Late Iron Age Scandinavia* (Oxford, UK: Oxbow Books, 2019), 30

Price even argues it is possible that additional, more mystical hamr existed as vessels for projecting one's power beyond their body, a claim that aligns somewhat with Perabo's observation of some figures being described as possessing more than one hamr.[28] These conceptions manifested in many ways in surviving myths, historical accounts, and archeological finds.

Myth and mysticism are the best starting points for understanding this concept of a malleable form that extended beyond one's body, beginning with shapeshifting. Changing form is, while not common, a frequent occurrence in the sagas, with beings of all kinds altering their forms either deliberately or otherwise, with some changes being more permanent than others. The two most obvious examples of such shape-changing among the gods are Odin and Loki, both of whom are notorious for taking on many different shapes in their stories, yet they are not alone in doing this. Freyja's falcon-feather cloak gives her the ability to take the shape of birds of prey, allowing her to fly across whole realms. Even Thor could be said to be engaging in a more limited example of shape-changing when he is disguised as Freyja in the Thrymskvitha to regain his hammer.[29]

These temporary changes in form operate in relationship with more permanent alterations, often the results of sacrifice, which reflect deeper shifts in the nature of the god in question. Odin's loss of an eye and hanging from the World Tree are easily two of the most well-known of such form- and Self-altering changes to a god's hamr in the sagas, though they are not alone. Tyr's sacrifice of his sword hand to bind down Fenrir represents a similar permanent change in hamr because of sacrifice. This loss becomes a part of who Tyr is and everything Tyr represents. Even Loki, though known as a master shapeshifter, sees permanent alterations to form following the shaving of Sif's hair. When the god of mischief's bet ended with the dvergr coming to claim their head, they claimed the dvergr had never asked for Loki's neck, so the master makers settled for stitching Loki's mouth shut. Loki's scars are often described by modern practitioners as one of the Catalyst's most distinguishing attributes.

Another form of shape-changer is the berserker. Berserkers were said to don the hides of bears, or wolves in the case of their ulfhednar cousins, to take

---

28. Price, *The Viking Way*, 30.

29. Perabo, "Shapeshifting in Old Nordic-Icelandic Literature," 136–38.

on the shape and might of these ferocious animals. In battle, these arts were said to grant berserkers immunity to pain, fearlessness, and unrelenting ferocity. Those who took on the shapes of these mighty animals were still seen as the same people even though their form was treated as transformed. In surviving written accounts, these fearsome warriors are something of a stock villain, a possible product of the shifts in power relationships in Nordic societies that saw a loss of standing among representations of a more animistic past at the expense of the rising warrior elite who often sponsored these epic poems. They further reinforce a strain of thought in pre-conversion societies that shows a clear understanding of the body as malleable and not a fixed, defined form.[30]

A clear example of these ideas in action can be found in the persistent evidence of body modification in pre-conversion Nordic societies. Historical sources describe how societies in Nordic Scandinavia engaged in different forms of tattooing. Though no direct physical evidence has survived, Ibn Fadlan's account of Swedish Vikings known as the Rus on the Baltic coast provides one of the best descriptions of Nordic tattooing. As Ibn Fadlan wrote, "Every man is tattooed from finger nails to neck with dark green (or green or blue-black) trees, figures."[31]

A further form of body modification found in the archaeological and textual sources was the engraving grooves into the teeth of Nordic warriors. In some accounts, these grooves were painted or dyed in vibrant colors. Others had specific shapes, designs, and patterns filed into their teeth, suggesting these are examples of a well-developed practice with a range of different expressive possibilities. This rather intense dental work, according to historical osteologist Caroline Arcini, was the product of very skilled labor and deliberate craft.[32]

---

30. Owen Rees, "Going Berserk: The Psychology of the Berserkers," *Medieval Warfare* 2, no. 1 (2012) 23–25; Neil Price, *Children of Ash and Elm: A History of the Vikings* (New York: Basic Books, 2020), 324–326.

31. H. M. Smyser, "Ibn Fadlan's Account of the Rus with Some Commentary and Some Allusions to Beowulf," in *Franciplegius: Medieval and Linguistic Studies in Honor of Francis Peabody Magoun Jr.*, ed. Jess B. Bessinger Jr. and Robert P. Creed (New York: New York University Press, 1965), 93.

32. Caroline Ahlstom Arcini, "The Vikings Bare Their Filed Teeth," *American Journal of Physical Anthropology* 128, no. 4 (2005): 727–33, doi:10.1002/ajpa.20164.

There is even evidence this malleability may have extended to their understanding of gender. One of the best archeological examples of this is the Birka warrior tomb, where a female skeleton was found with the full honors and accoutrements of a male warrior chieftain. Archeologist Neil Price argues this particular find provides concrete proof of these particular Nordic peoples having an understanding of gender that was not rooted in human biology but rather in how a person lived in society. The Birka grave, according to Price, could represent a person whom modern practitioners might describe as everything from a masculine-presenting woman to a trans man or genderfluid.[33] When these documented tendencies are taken in conjunction with folklore surrounding shape-shifting, it is certainly appropriate to view the hamr as a malleable canvas. Hamr is form that can be altered according to your desires through temporary and more enduring forms of self-expression and personal fulfillment.[34]

Hugr

Next, if one follows in the footsteps of the body-mind duality, is hugr. This word is often translated as "mind" or "thought." Thought, as a distinct thing unto itself, runs deep throughout the lore. It first reaches humanity as one of the gifts given by Odin, Hoenir, and Lodur:

Soul they had not, sense they had not,	Önd þau ne áttu, óð þau ne höfðu,
Heat nor motion, nor goodly hue;	lá né læti né litu góða;
Soul gave Othin, sense gave Hönir,	önd gaf Óðinn, óð gaf Hœnir,
Heat gave Lothur and goodly hue.[35]	lá gaf Lóðurr ok litu góða.[36]

---

33. Price, *Children of Ash and Elm*, 177.

34. Meilan Solly, "What Ötzi the Iceman's Tattoos Reveal About Copper Age Medical Practices." *Smithsonian*, September 10, 2018. https://www.smithsonianmag.com /smart-news/what-otzi-icemans-tattoos-reveal-about-copper-age-medical-practices -180970244/.

35. Bellows, *Poetic Edda*, Voluspo 18.

36. "Konungsbók eddukvæða GKS 2365 4to," Stofnun Árna Magnússonar, accessed December 16, 2022, https://www.arnastofnun.is/is/konungsbok-eddukvaeda-gks-2365 -4to.

Oð, translated by Henry Adams Bellows as "sense," is also rendered by linguists as meaning "mind" and in the verb form refers to an almost divine state of ecstasy with connotations of madness, inspiration, and frenzy.[37] These connotations strongly suggest that the mind was seen as more than just one's internal thought processes and perspectives but also the kind of frenzied, excited inspiration that drives creativity and understanding. This is also seen in Fire and Ice practice as support for including intuition and emotion as part of the hugr.

Along with the gifts of breath from Odin and the flush of life from Hoenir and Loðurr, the three gods gave direction to Ask and Embla in the Voluspo, transforming two trees without fate into beings with deliberate will and the power to act on it. This places hugr in relationship with hamr, hamingja, and fylgja while also keeping it a distinct thing of its own.[38]

Even though hugr was tied to the other parts of the Self, it is capable of moving independently of the larger whole. Tales of seers and witches casting their minds far from their forms to observe distant events abound in the lore, with the Havamal even listing a spell for severing these wandering eavesdroppers from their forms:

> A tenth I know, what time I see
> House-riders flying on high;
> So I can work that wildly they go,
> Showing their true shapes,
> Hence to their own homes.[39]

Of all the parts of the self, hugr is probably the closest in Nordic practice to the modern concept of the soul, as the clearest representation of conscious, deliberate will of the individual does share some resemblance to the Christian soul. Price's conception of the hugr emphasizes this understanding of hugr as personal essence, citing the case of King Atli's description in the Volsungasaga as having a "wolfish soul."[40] Cat Heath describes this as an essential component

---

37. Andy Orchard, *Dictionary of Norse Myth and Legend* (London: Cassell: 1997), 121.

38. Vladimir E. Orel, *A Handbook of Germanic Etymology* (Leiden, Netherlands: Brill, 2003), 469.

39. Bellows, *Poetic Edda*, Havamal 156.

40. Price, *The Viking Way*, 31.

to what she calls the "free soul" empowered by Odin's gift of breath and possessing this intrinsic ability to move freely from the body's limitations.[41] It is also, in Fire and Ice practice, the element of the Self that persists after death in the Otherworlds such as Helheim and Valhalla or stalking places familiar to them in life. How the hugr is different is there is no strong implication of it being superior to the other four, even though it is the source of thought, memory, and consciousness. Hugr's capacity to wander forth may even extend to the hugr of gods if, as is suggested by Neil price, you view Odin's ravens, Huginn and Muninn, as projections of the many-named god's mind.[42]

Fylgja

Next closest to hugr is the fylgja (plural *fylgjur*), which is referred to sometimes in Fire and Ice practice as your spiritual shadow and is also often referred to as a fetch in many sources. Price describes the historical fylgja as being very strongly independent while still being connected to a person, with some even being passed down through family lines or even rejecting the person they are associated with in extreme cases.[43] Often depicted as animals, though some take more human shapes, these beings are said to have a will and a mind of their own independent of hugr. Fylgjur, according to Cat Heath, cannot travel freely, possess their own autonomy, and are prone to wandering of their own accord. She further argues that many instances of people encountering their fylgja were omens of death.[44]

There is some similarity between the idea of the fylgja and concepts such as familiars or guardian spirits. What sets the fylgja apart from these concepts is how intimately connected the fylgja is to the person. A fylgja, unlike familiars or guardian spirits, is a more direct manifestation of an individual even though they have a significant degree of autonomy. In Fire and Ice practice, fylgjur are often understood as a manifestation of something similar to your subconscious mind, or what Freud refers to as the id. This tension of independence

41. Cat Heath, *Elves, Witches & Gods: Spinning Old Heathen Magic in the Modern Day,* (Woodbury, MN: Llewellyn Worldwide, 2011), 96–97.

42. Price, *Children of Ash and Elm,* 44.

43. Price, *The Viking Way,* 30

44. Heath, *Elves, Witches & Gods,* 96–97.

and intimate connection make your fylgja an excellent guide, protector, and sounding board that can be reached through meditative practices like what is outlined in the exercise at the end of this chapter.

Fylgjur are the aspect of the Self that is most directly connected to mystical practices in Radical Heathenry. As an intimately connected being who exists outside of the limitations of form and mind, a person's fylgja knows them as well as they know themselves. Their autonomy means they often have their own perspectives on whatever may be facing you, making your fylgja an ideal guide during ecstatic and seiðr workings. They can be a useful sounding board as well, prompting you to consider other options or paths that could be considered. You could almost see the fylgja, in this aspect, as similar to the proverbial shoulder angel and devil, though in this case it would be less Biblical and more naturalistic, Nordic, singular, and personal. The honesty of your fylgja often sinks deep, being founded in their unique relationship with your decisions and actions.

Hamingja

After fylgja, hugr, and hamr, hamingja is probably the most nebulous of the parts of the Self. Often translated as "luck," hamingja is far more expansive in the source material than being a manifestation of one's good fortune. In historical sources, hamingja takes on a critical role.[45] Thomas Dubois describes the hamingja as a guardian spirit who has considerable power to shape the fortunes of the people they watch over, with some described as being hereditary and carrying luck through the generations.[46] For Neil Price, a hamingja was more than a guardian spirit and could be understood as the personification of a person's luck that could be perceived clearly by those who were trained in the proper arts for doing so.[47] What remains consistent, regardless of specific interpretation, is the clear relationship between hamingja, luck, and what this meant for an individual's ability to shape the world around them.

---

45. Thomas A. Dubois, *Nordic Religions in the Viking Age* (Philadelphia: University of Pennsylvania Press, 1999), 52.

46. Dubois, *Nordic Religions in the Viking Age*, 188.

47. Price, *The Viking Way*, 30.

Hamingja is probably the most heavily discussed, analyzed, and debated component of the Self in Heathenry. Many different perspectives on this topic exist, with most agreeing that hamingja as an aspect of Self represents a very personal form of luck that was passed down from previous generations.

Even though hamingja is defined by your ørlog, it is also something that can grow, shrink, be cultivated, and be lost depending on what you do and how you utilize your luck. Hamingja, as an aspect of Self, has a durability not present in the other components that, along with its role as personification of luck, sets it apart from the rest of the Self. Hamingja, as a Radical part of Self, is the embodiment of your capacity to cause change and is a constant reminder how the fruit of our deeds endures in the world beyond us.[48]

As was discussed somewhat in chapter 2, hamingja has a very complex relationship with wyrd. Its capacity to influence ørlog, through deliberate action, is simultaneously shaped by how ørlog defines the limits of every person's hamingja. Nothing better emphasizes this element than how hamingja is treated in the source material as hereditary, with children inheriting their hamingja from their parents and passing it on to those who follow in their footsteps.[49] This puts hamingja squarely at the crossroads between ørlog, personal choice, and wyrd, making it the element of the Self that is most directly connected to change and the world around you.

One of the most important concepts to consider when discussing or using hamingja is its transferability. Hamingja, in the source material, can potentially be shared with others through the bestowing of luck, favor, and support both in terms of the actions taken by the person offering such support and on a more metaphysical, intangible level through the sharing of power.[50] This transferability also strongly implies that it is quite possible for many people to pool their hamingja in pursuit of a shared goal or objective, granting them all the collective capacity to reshape or even undo ørlog that may normally be well beyond the power of any individual. In Radical Heathenry, this pooling of power manifests both metaphysically, such as during workings or ritual, and

---

48. Heath, *Elves, Witches & Gods*, 92–94; Lafayllve, *A Practical Heathen's Guide to Asatru*, 60, 230.

49. Dubois, *Nordic Religions in the Viking Age*, 188.

50. Bettina Sejbjerg Sommer, "The Norse Concept of Luck," *Scandinavian Studies* 79, no. 3 (Fall 2007): 281, 292–93.

more concretely, through the shared power that comes from group cooperation and coordination. For Fire and Ice practitioners, this aspect of hamingja is validation of the power of collective, cooperative action to bring about change in the world both great and small.

rite

LENDING LUCK

The following rite is an example of how a modern practitioner can extend their hamingja to those in need. It only requires a prepared offering that can include poetic verses, works of art, or other valued possessions offered as sacrifice. As with all rites, you must follow through with actions that will make your desired outcome more likely to pass. Be careful to only give a small portion of your luck, as giving too much all at once can have unexpected consequences.

rite

Begin by invoking Fire and Ice to set the space with the rite in chapter 1.

Clearly focus on the person you wish to lend your luck to. This can be done with mental visualization or by using a picture of them. Speak all the names by which you know them, including any personal nicknames and online aliases.

Name the thing, person, or circumstances they are currently facing.

Bring forth the offering or, if it is a verse, speak it. Breathe a portion of your luck into the offering, visualizing a small piece of this energy entering into the offering. Say, "With this offering, I lend a part of my luck to aid [the beneficiary's name] in their plight!"

Sacrifice and dispose of the offering. Release the luck imbued in the rite with a puff of breath.

The Heathen Self and the Modern World

This four-part model of the Self, built on complex, cooperative relationships between coequal components, presents a direct challenge to many of the assumptions that run strongly through modern life. Two areas where the Radical Heathen understanding of the Self especially conflict are how the world understands the relationships between body and individual and how it understands the relationships between the individual and the world around them. These concepts are known as biological determinism and atomization.

Biological determinism is the idea that your body and personhood are shaped by inescapable biological truths, such as physical sex, which reach to the depths of who you are.[51] This concept has played a significant role in shaping how we understand ourselves and our place in society by, among other things, hardcoding different activities, pastimes, and work to specific gender norms and roles.[52] When put hand in hand with ideas such as God's will, the result is a highly deterministic understanding of how personhood operates that greatly diminishes the role of individual agency, choice, and freedom. Such notions of bodily and personal rigidity defined by forces beyond one's control cage the individual in a place of submission to these forces, replacing the potential of relationship with a reality of unalterable obedience.

This is further exacerbated by what is known as atomization, the tendency to treat each person as an isolated individual unto themselves, deny the importance of social relations and collective action, and force people to view possible avenues for changing their conditions solely through the perspective of the individual.[53] This reduction of the person into a lone island unto themselves

---

51. Stephen J. Gould, *Ever Since Darwin: Reflections in Natural History* (New York: W. W. Norton and Company, 1977), 254–56.

52. W. Carson Byrd and Matthew W. Hughey, "Born that Way? 'Scientific' Racism Is Creeping Back into Our Thinking. Here's What to Watch Out For," *Washington Post*, September 28, 2015, https://www.washingtonpost.com/news/monkey-cage/wp/2015/09/28/born-that-way-scientific-racism-is-creeping-back-into-our-thinking-heres-what-to-watch-out-for; Prerna Singh, "How Biological Determinism Perpetuates Sexism Using 'Science,'" Feminism in India, June 18, 2018, https://feminisminindia.com/2018/06/18/biological-determinism-science-sexism/.

53. Tim Adams, "Anxious, Atomised...and Not in It Together: The State of Britain in 2015," *The Guardian*, April 19, 2015, https://www.theguardian.com/society/2015/apr/19/anxious-atomised-not-in-it-together-the-state-of-britain-2015.

depends on the active denial of any kind of deeper, more meaningful relation-ships with the broader world around them or even within themselves despite evidence to the contrary. This crude severing of connection leaves the modern person standing alone against the world with only their own individual capac-ity available to them as the means to bring about any sort of change to their circumstances.[54] What makes this process worse is this hyperisolation promises greater personal freedom while actively reducing your ability to act on the so-cial institutions that define the modern world. When your primary means of interacting with and effecting the world is limited to your individual choices, then other possibilities, including those offered by collective action, are effec-tively foreclosed at the outset.

This first question of how this understanding interacts with more rigid, bi-ologically determined models of the person and self that are common in the modern world strikes at the heart of how the individual is understood in the world. Most people in Christian-influenced parts of the world operate based on a very strong sense of body-mind dualism or a similar body-mind-spirit trichot-omy that sees the core components as joined yet inherently different, separate, and operating in a hierarchical fashion where the mind or soul, depending on the variation, is in charge.[55] Such notions of personhood make the body into a plaything of the "true" driver of your life instead of being a necessary, coequal component in what makes you who you are.

Each of these elements, as critical as they are to understanding the modern person, is deeply at odds with the horizontal, malleable, and deeply intercon-nected Heathen Self. On the question of society's views of the person, body, mind, and soul there are some clear surface-level differences, yet what these points of conflict imply runs much deeper than having a different philosoph-ical understanding of personhood. The same is true of the four-part Self and the phenomenon of atomization, particularly since the Heathen Self exists in a state of inseparable relationships with the broader world.

---

54. Jared Keller, "Americans Are Staying as Far Away from Each Other as Possible," Pacific Standard, last modified June 14, 2017, https://psmag.com/social-justice/americans-are -staying-as-far-away-from-each-other-as-possible.

55. ReligiousTolerance, "About the Soul," accessed June 11, 2022, https://www.religious tolerance.org/souldef.htm; Howard Robinson, "Dualism," Stanford Encyclopedia of Philosophy, revised September 1, 2020, https://plato.stanford.edu/entries/dualism/.

Understanding the Individual

The four-part Self in Fire and Ice practice deeply clashes with rigid, biologically dictated models of self while also loudly refusing to conform to an atomized understanding of the individual. What makes this particularly essential is many of the assumptions baked into these models must be undone as part of developing a sustaining relationship with the Self and all its components.

Of these modern frameworks, the best to start grappling with regards questions of body, mind, and soul. Thanks to these frameworks, we live in a society whose Western-defined understanding of the person is strongly primed toward atomization and isolation. One can argue this is because, in many ways, the modern body and mind or body, mind, and soul maps of the person function on assumptions that place one aspect superior to all others, with the rest shoved into subordinate roles. This understanding of the individual also, inherently, assumes a level of contradiction and conflict between these different aspects. Nothing better sums up this attitude than the common narrative of people being torn between their base desires and their higher selves, an assumption that pits body against mind and soul in an endless battle over right and wrong. This whole conflict's parallel between heaven and hell or obedience to the will of divinity versus rebellion against it are inescapable, as are prevailing highly Christian notions of bodily desires being at odds with the aspirations of the soul or pursuits of the mind.

Many of these models of a conflicted, warring individual also assume an understanding of personhood that crowns biology as king. Nothing better expresses this than traditional gender roles that slot everyone into male and female boxes with little, if any, room for exceptions. These roles include typecast jobs, social functions, and expected patterns of behavior, such as general acceptance of male aggression in contrast with female submission or the association of physically demanding activities with masculinity in contrast to more domestically associated feminine labor. All these models draw their legitimacy from a biologically framed understanding of reality that, historically speaking, only came into existence within the past five centuries and utilizes examples from prior periods to justify its validity. This came following a period of concentrated argument for our diametrically male-female world, as described by Thomas Laqueur, and was implemented by what feminist theorist Silvia Federici appropriately describes as brutal, dehumanizing violence.[56] These frameworks further dictated what bodies and forms could do with an eye toward what was seen as best for increasing productivity as much as possible.

The four-part Self very clearly does not conform to this understanding of the individual or the form they take. The Self's nature as a collection of elements working in conjunction as part of a greater whole is nothing like entirely too many conceptions of the individual that pit body in conflict with mind and soul. There simply appears to be no reference to such a concern in surviving source material, with the demands of honor, luck, and fate weighing far more heavily on the minds of the figures of the sagas than an eternal tug of war between base and exalted desires.

The same is true of biologically cast gender constructions that place anything defined as feminine at the service of what is narrowly constructed as acceptably masculine. There are, contrary to many modern myths regarding early medieval period and its peoples, considerable examples of women in pre-conversion Scandinavia managing vast estates, ruling over early kingdoms, and even taking to the battlefield.

The recent reexamination of the famous Birka tomb in Sweden, which concluded its assumed male warrior occupant was anatomically female, is one of the most famous examples of strong deviations from allegedly traditional gender norms.[57] These seemingly firm, inviolable boundaries are further challenged by the plethora of form-changing gods, heroes, and metaphysics that merrily blur the lines between gender norms. Simply put, there is more than enough in the surviving source material that thoroughly repudiates any notion of conventional gender roles as being universal, ancient, or pervasive in the human experience.

Economic Exchanges

This same stark relief is apparent when you turn to social atomization and the modern world's tendency to treat every person as a lone island whose

---

56. Thomas Laqueur, *Making Sex: Body and Gender from the Greeks to Freud* (Cambridge, MA: Harvard University Press, 1990), 3–7; Silvia Federici, *Caliban and the Witch: Women, the Body, and Primitive Accumulation* (Brooklyn, NY: Autonomedia, 2004), 14–17.

57. Neil Price et al., "Viking Warrior Women? Reassessing Birka Chamber Grave Bj.581," *Antiquity* 93, no. 367 (February 2019): 189–93, doi:10.15184/aqy.2018.258.

relationships are reduced to a series of economic exchanges. Thanks to this accelerating tendency toward social breakdown, anything resembling shared common spaces defined by community need instead of commercial gain are disappearing, with all that remains coming with increasingly steep price tags. Personal identity, at least in the eyes of the marketplace, has increasingly been reduced to a series of consumer choices, brands, and media preferences.

Even religious practice, both mainstream and underground, is being reduced to how you purchase instead of how you pray, as shown by everything from the explosion of Christian prosperity gospel, complete with megachurches built in dead shopping malls, to Sephora's cosmetic "Starter Witch Kits."[58] This transmutation of the social into quick cash is, in part, rooted in the denial of any nontransactional approach to human relationships. Far from exalting the individual, this steady diminishing of every form of interaction down to dollars, cents, and brands hollows out the lived experience.

Therefore, it begs the question what the Heathen Self offers in response to such an abrasive understanding of the person. For modern practitioners, the Heathen Self presents a clear alternative to an increasingly commodified view of people and their place in existence thanks to its deep roots in a complex system of interdependence. These relationships weave throughout the fabric of reality, binding everything and everyone together. This truth of interconnection is as present within how the individual is understood as it is in how the individual's relationships with the world function. To put it simply, the Self's foundation on relationships, from the ground up, is completely at odds with social atomization.

---

58. Louisa Kroll, "Megachurches, Megabusinesses," *Forbes*, September 17, 2003, https://www.forbes.com/2003/09/17/cz_lk_0917megachurch.html?sh=2e6f55d27489; Ruth Graham, "Can Megachurches Deal with Mega Money in a Christian Way?" *Atlantic*, March 12, 2014, https://www.theatlantic.com/business/archive/2014/03/can-megachurches-deal-with-mega-money-in-a-christian-way/284379/; Kate Taylor, "Thousands of Americans Are Going to Church in Dead Malls," Business Insider, June 19, 2017, https://www.businessinsider.com/dying-malls-are-being-transformed-into-churches-2017-6; Lauren Strapagiel, "That 'Starter Witch Kit' Was Canceled After Massive Backlash on Social Media," BuzzFeed News, September 6, 2018, https://www.buzzfeednews.com/article/laurenstrapagiel/sephora-starter-witch-kit-pinrose-white-sage.

This begins at the personal level. Just as this model of the individual as a set of equal components working together to form the greater Self stands in stark contrast to the implied hierarchies and struggles inherent in body-mind dualism, the same is true of when the Self encounters the problem of social atomization. You cannot argue that a person is an isolated entity unto themselves who is most defined by their consumer choices when your philosophical and metaphysical understanding of the individual rests on this foundation. When relationship is the glue that makes you who you are, it is simply not possible to strip this away with any amount of microtargeting, valorization of more toxic forms of individualism, or exaltation of superficial brands and products. Doing so requires denying the very fabric of the Self, robbing it of what it needs most to be healthy and fully functional.

Extending this logic outward to the social only reinforces this line of reasoning. Just as the elements of the Self only create a fully realized person when they work together, the same is true of these elements and the Self in relation with society.

Hugr and hamr, for one example, are both defined as much by a person's internal drives as they are by how they relate to the world around them. Hugr's role as the processor of information and projector of the personality during seiðr exists in constant relationship with the world around it. Hamr, similarly, operates in relationship with everything around the Self no matter what form it takes on. Much of the form-changing described in surviving source material has as clear an impact on how people respond to the form-changer as it does on how the form-shifted work with the world around them. In some cases, such as the suppression of the berserker cults, operating in this framework of understanding put people directly at odds with changing social orders who saw this potential as threatening to their power.

Exploration of hamingja and fylgja, the more metaphysical elements of the Self, shows a similar pattern. Hamingja, at its core, is defined by those who came before you and is constantly shaped by a person's choices interacting with the ørlog of the world around them. Nothing better reinforces this than hamingja's transferable and collective properties, both of which show how much it exists in a very social context. Fylgja, similarly, shows a side of the Self that is simultaneously deeply personal and deeply relational in nature. Their place as a guide for the Self, in life and mystical workings, is rooted in the fylgja's own relationships with the world around you. Whether you view these elements in a more secular or heavily mystical frame, there is no question they both reinforce how much the elements of the Self operate in relationship with the broader world as opposed to being components operating in isolation.

What this all ultimately argues is the Nordic and Radical Heathen understandings of how the individual works are strongly at odds with deeply held, sometimes unquestioned frameworks that are responsible for holding up society as we know it. Ideas such as body-mind dualism, biological determinism, and social atomization are concepts that have no place in this deeply relational, cooperative approach to understanding the individual. Their limitations, harmful effects, and clear contradictions are obstacles to be overcome during the processes of realizing the elements of the Self, what they mean for you, and how you work with them. Any efforts to develop the Self and its components will depend as much on dismantling these narratives as they do on cultivating your inner relationships. Only by tackling the challenges presented by these old bones is it possible to craft a new world of personal understanding, autonomy, and sustaining fulfillment.

Doing the Work of the Self

Whether you view the four-part Self from a more mystical or secular perspective, contemplating the implications, connections, and relationships of hugr, hamr, hamingja, and fylgja can help you better understand yourself. Working to understand these different aspects of what makes you who you are provides a more complete, grounded set of perspectives that focuses on relationship and connection as opposed to hierarchy and power. From a more metaphysical perspective, such work is vital, as each of these different aspects of Self plays a critical role in Fire and Ice mystical practices.

Each aspect of the Self carries its own challenges and possibilities, each of which must be navigated as part of an ongoing process. Above all else, do not be discouraged if you encounter difficulties, blocks, or other obstacles during these processes. The work of Self is labor that is constant and everyone, no matter how great their current level of understanding, had to begin in the same place of inexperience, uncertainty, and ignorance.

Hugr is a solid place to start this exploration of Selfwork, particularly because it is the part of the Self that is closest to your perspective and experiences.

As the filter for consciousness, hugr directly shapes how you understand, perceive, and interpret the world around you. This, therefore, argues that working with your hugr is centered on first understanding how your mind influences your comprehension of what is around you. For a modern reader, this may carry with it implications of intelligence, learning, and other similar concepts thanks to how all these concepts are directly linked to the mind in much of society. For Radical Heathens, much of the core work of hugr lies more in understanding perceptions, discernment, and taking care of your mental and emotional health.

Understanding your assumptions, biases, and prejudices is one of the first essential steps in building a solid relationship with your hugr. Everyone, regardless of where they come from or how they lived, carries their own biases and assumptions. Contrary to the claims of many vocal rationalists, ranging from New Atheists to right-wing internet grifters, there is no magical, self-evident formula of logic and reason that makes this go away. This is because many of these biases are the products of personal experiences, some of which are influenced to varying degrees by traumatic events. Sometimes these biases are well-founded with clear, supported reasons for existing while others may be the results of faulty information, snap assumptions, or succumbing to the demands of group pressures to better fit in. Recognizing our biases, how they developed, and if they are based on our lived experience is essential to working and understanding our hugr.

Addressing your personal biases helps lay the foundation for cultivating the skills that make up what is often referred to as discernment. This is the ability to accurately and consistently assess what is happening around you, especially when you may be experiencing otherworldly or wyrd phenomena. In life, generally, everyone is assailed by multiple competing flows of information, stimuli, and responses that often make comprehending what is happening around you a challenging process. This is part of why understanding your biases is an important element of developing solid discernment but is also only a first step in a lifelong process. Discernment, at least in this context, depends heavily on consistently and reliably asking yourself to trust yet verify that what happened to you did, indeed, happen as you experienced it.

In many instances in daily life, this is not likely to be a consistent problem for most. Much of what people experience in waking life is usually as it appears to be with no deeper or more complex explanation needed. Embracing this and reinforcing it by applying Occam's razor, a logical frame that argues the explanations that fit all available information and rely on the least number of assumptions are often the most accurate ones, is an important step in this process. When it becomes essential is in times of disagreement, confusion, or experiences with the Powers. These are instances when you may doubt your perception of events, question the information being relayed through your hugr, and wonder if what you are experiencing is indeed what is actually happening.

In times of such uncertainty, it is often best to first seek verification for what happened. This can be everything from checking in with a trusted friend to seeking further clarification from the person you are in disagreement with if possible and examining any available records or documentation, such as video or audio recordings, that could confirm or deny particular details and possibilities. If this trust-but-verify process provides the necessary explanation for dispelling any uncertainties, which can potentially mean determining the person you are arguing with is acting in bad faith or proving the highly unexpected, stressful accident you saw did happen, then no further examination is necessary. Sometimes this could mean you stumble onto a deeper, more complex set of explanations for what you experienced but these, again, can be subjected to the same pattern of trust but verify.

When, however, you experience something otherworldly, mystical, or that seems to be of the Powers, this can be a more complicated and often challenging process. What makes this process truly fraught and difficult is how much of modern society dismisses phenomena such as direct mystical experiences during trancework, synchronicity in the form of seemingly mundane events that have a clear otherworldly character, or even more physical manifestations as everything from the products of an overly active imagination to symptoms of mental illness. This consistent tendency in society to dismiss such experiences out of hand carries its own influences, ranging from an almost knee-jerk skepticism to doubting one's mental health, all of which may raise further barriers to spiritual experiences. Even so, it is still necessary to know the difference between something that may just be in your head and one that is coming from somewhere else.

How you respond will vary depending on the nature of the experience, but what is most consistent is to first, paraphrasing Arthur Conan Doyle, determine what mundane explanations may exist for what you have encountered.[59] Anything that is probable or possible, from a cat knocking over a cup in the next room to a consistent weather pattern, should be first considered when discussing encounters with what could potentially be the Powers or signs of their presence. You should only begin questioning if what you experienced was otherworldly if the mundane explanations do not fully account for what was experienced. Even if this is the case, it is important to entertain multiple possible explanations and meanings from what you experience. Part of the art of discernment lies not just in ascertaining what may or may not be true but in also being able to assess multiple, competing explanations for a scenario and determining which are most sufficient and compelling as explanations.

The final facet of the work of hugr is taking care of your mental health. There are many ways the modern world assails your mental and emotional state, ranging from the daily stresses on the job to the more existential crises that hang ever closer over all heads these days. This is further complicated by the many ways people's minds work, ranging from significantly different perspectives to the multitude of neurodivergent patterns. All of this urges that you find ways to mitigate, cope with, or seek resolution to these stressors for your hugr to remain healthy, able to understand what is happening in the world, and best guide you. When doing so, please seek out the advice and assistance of a certified mental health practitioner who is accepting of your core values, particularly whatever spirituality you practice. Such counsel is invaluable, though it is often challenging for many Heathens and Pagans to find therapists who are accepting of more unconventional forms of spiritual practice and experiences.

Working with your hamr follows broadly similar principles, though the specifics are adapted to the particulars that are unique to hamr. A significant part of doing the work of the hamr, like the hugr, depends on unraveling many assumptions regarding the physical form imposed by modern society. The essence of this work lies in returning to a state of accepting your form's malleability and finding ways to make your hamr match how you feel you should manifest in the world. In summary, these can be described as understanding what makes you comfortable in your own form, understanding how your form

---

59. Arthur Conan Doyle, *The Sign of the Four*, in *Lippincott's Monthly Magazine* (London: Spencer Blackett, 1890), chap. 6.

influences your relationship with the world around you, and remembering the importance of self-care.

Becoming comfortable in your form is the cornerstone of all work with your hamr. This is a process which will, unquestionably, unfold over the course of your entire life and see its own ups, downs, and doldrums along the way. Regardless of the obstacles, what matters most is you always strive to bring your hamr into a shape that most closely matches what you think best reflects who you are. If it is necessary to change your body to make this happen, even in permanent ways, then that is part of what needs to be done for your hamr to be more in alignment with your vision for it. If there are aspects that are already pleasing to you and who it is you want to be, then keep them, regardless of how these may be perceived or dismissed by others. What matters most is that hamr reflects your desires and not those imposed by others upon you.

Hand in hand with the process of becoming comfortable within your form is understanding how alterations to it, both big and small, may change how people respond to you in society. Everything from shifts in posture and body language to totally different clothing, body modifications such as piercings and tattoos, or gender confirmation will inevitably change how people respond to you. Understanding how this works for you is something that will involve some experimentation and exploration, ranging from the seemingly mundane act of donning workplace attire to more dramatic or permanent changes. These discoveries can help you understand both how you can change the way you present and act in space to directly impact how you are received whether your goal is to seize every eye in the room, blend in with the shadows, or something else entirely. Some of the more spectacular transformations in the lore, such as Loki form-shifting into a horse or Freyja taking the shape of a falcon, are well beyond what is physically possible at the time of this writing. More subtle examples, such as Odin's many different varieties of mysterious traveler, are well within the realm of possibility.

Regardless of how deeply you work with your hamr, it is essential that you take care of your body and practice good self-care. This means listening to your form when you are stressed, pushing the limits of your capabilities, or under significant pressure. Many a serious injury or ailment has been avoided by taking the time to listen to what your body is telling you, slow down, or otherwise give yourself the space to rest and recover from strain more fully. Unfortunately, many people do not have the space or time to properly do this on a regular basis, a problem best summarized by how many may consider such essential time an unaffordable luxury. Regardless of your circumstances, everyone needs rest, self-care, and time to relax even though the means to properly do this are constrained by the demands of modern life. However you make space for it, give yourself such necessary rest and be sure to consult qualified health professionals on what may work best given your particular circumstances.

Hamingja, in contrast to hamr and hugr, is much broader in scope and shape. As it represents your full ability to influence the world around you, hamingja can take on many different forms and manifest in many different and at times seemingly contradictory or mysterious ways. Hamingja's transferable properties makes such work especially vital, as it helps you understand both what you can do with your hamingja and how it can be used to shape the world around you. Working with your hamingja challenges you to consider how you influence the world around you, moments when you or others have taken collective action to cause change, and how your life experiences have shaped your ability to influence the world.

How you influence the world around you often takes on many different forms. In cases where a person holds a position of clear power and authority, this is easy to understand, as their influence radiates outward from these institutional supports. For most people, however, this is not always as obvious as it could be. If you are working an unforgiving retail job, grinding away for finals, or otherwise living what many would call an ordinary life, it is easy to dismiss hamingja as an esoteric justification for power imbalances. Deeper self-reflection, however, can reveal how your hamingja shapes the world in ways both great and small. A good place to start is by recalling a time when your actions had a significant positive impact on another person's life. Think about how your actions did this, whether it was through persuasive words, a kind gesture, or something as simple as being present and supportive for them. Next, move mentally outward from this moment into how this person's life progressed with consideration for the influence of your actions. It is both in the immediate moment of exercising your unique capacities and the consequences that flow from them that your hamingja manifested.

This same process works equally well, with even more compelling results, when you apply it to instances of collective action. To do this, you can choose to either think back to an instance in your life when you and several other people came together to achieve a shared goal. Reflect on how each person's particular strengths and shortcomings played off one another, building to a stronger collective outcome where the capacity of the whole was greater than the sum of its parts. For further consideration, look up some historical examples when people with limited resources overcame great obstacles and won great battles through collective struggle. It is these moments, along with more personal ones, that show both the transferability of hamingja and its ability to be collectively pooled by many to achieve a far greater range of potential than any individual involved possessed.

The next step in developing awareness of your hamingja is reflecting on how your life experiences that make up your personal ørlog have shaped the ways you interact with the world. Understanding this personal ørlog, which plays a vital role in shaping your hamingja, is essential for developing a deeper relationship with your personal power. Consider, for example, how existing social institutions may have denied you opportunities that were open to others and how you responded to these moments of refusal or how you were able to make options for yourself despite such limitations. It is in these moments of adaptation and change that you would have shaped how your hamingja interacts with the world, effectively "making your own luck," as the popular expression implies. From there, move outward from the choices made to the skills that were required to do this, considering particularly what you cultivated within yourself and your life to make such change possible.

Fylgja, finally, represents what is probably the most esoteric element of the Radical Heathen Self. Working with the fylgja is the work of plumbing the depths of your subconscious, engaging your deepest desires, and developing a relationship with your spiritual shadow. This work, like all other aspects of working with the parts of the Self, is a constant and ongoing process especially because your fylgja has a mind of its own. Just as you change, grow, and develop, so too does your fylgja. At the conclusion of this chapter is an exercise meant to help you better work with your fylgja and create a direct connection with this aspect of Self.

One of the first things that will probably surprise you about your fylgja is their appearance. Though there are many descriptions of fylgjur in surviving source material, there is no consistency to how they were depicted or seen as manifesting. Some are described as animals, while others are depicted as human-like guardians. What they all share is a deep connection to the person they are associated with; beyond that, their forms vary just as widely as the diversity of the human experience. Therefore, you should not make any assumptions about how your fylgja should or should not look. Their form is a reflection of how they think, feel, and work along with being a manifestation of your more subconscious thoughts and desires.

Just as a fylgja will take any number of forms, the same is true of their personalities. Unlike the other parts of the Self, fylgjur have very definite agency both in historical source material and the experiences of modern practitioners. This makes them valuable guides during journeywork, but it also means they often have their own ideas regarding the best ways to approach and solve particular problems. As such, cultivating an effective relationship with your fylgja depends as much on establishing a solid metaphysical connection with them as it does on learning how to communicate with them, resolve disagreements, and come to a workable consensus. In some ways, working with a fylgja can be like developing a relationship with any of the Powers, though your fylgja, unlike a god or alfar, also knows you better than anything else ever could.

exercise
MEETING YOUR FYLGJA

The purpose of this exercise is to help the practitioner get in touch with their fylgja, the spiritual shadow self. Getting in touch with your fylgja is an important first step in developing self-work. Your fylgja can also be a very useful guide when doing forms of seiðr, such as utiseta and other meditative work.

Begin with the Understanding the Breath exercise that is in appendix I. When you have finished your breath cycles, do the Calming the Sea and Sky exercise also found in appendix I.

Sit in the state of calm that follows the Calming the Sea and Sky exercise for nine natural breaths.

Visualize your Self seated in front of a pool of water. Let the pool settle until it clearly shows your reflection. Reach into the pool and tap the surface. Let your reflection melt into the ripples and lose form.

Wait until the ripples cease and the pool becomes reflective again. Let the fragments of your old reflection take whatever shape comes most naturally. Leave your mind to float freely as it ripples, leaving the pool space to let a new form surface.

Give yourself a moment to take in every detail of the new form that is now in the pool of water. It might take on an animal shape or appear like an ancestor. Pay particular attention to the most distinctive details, like the color of an animal fylgja's fur or a distinctive item of clothing worn by a human fylgja. These specific details make it easier to remember and connect with your fylgja during meditation.

Watch as your fylgja steps out of the pool and listen to whatever it has to say or show you.

When you are finished interacting with your fylgja, let it walk back into the pool, dissolving back into your reflection.

Take nine deep breaths. As you breathe in, focus more on your body and the space around you. On the ninth breath, open your eyes and take some time to reflect on what you experienced.

chapter four
THE WORLD TREE

Mimameith its name, and no one knows
What root beneath it runs;
And few can guess what shall fell the tree,
For iron nor fire shall fell it.
—Svipdagsmal 30, *Poetic Edda*

The heart of all the Nordic Pagan cosmos is the World Tree, the central pillar of reality. It is both the core of a vast, multiversal ecosystem and the vital connecting tissue responsible for binding the layers of existence together. All the Nine Worlds of Nordic reality, including physical existence as we know it, depend on the World Tree for their existence. Everything, from the fiery depths of Muspelheim to the towering halls of Asgard, rests on the World Tree's mighty branches. When the fires of Ragnarök consume the Tree, they will engulf everything on the Tree, reducing all forms of existence to a cinder. It stands at the crossroads of all existence, representing an all-encompassing organic order to existence. If there was any one image, mythic symbol, or reference that could truly sum up the essence of Nordic-inspired practice, it would be this vast entity's mighty trunk, towering branches, and burrowing roots.

One intriguing riddle that heightens one's sense of awe and mystery around the World Tree is how no surviving source gives its name. The two surviving names in the *Poetic Edda* for it are themselves kennings and not direct descriptions or representations of the tree. The well-known *Yggdrasil*, "Ygg's Steed," refers to when Odin hung from the tree for nine days and nights in pursuit of knowledge and wisdom. The less commonly used term *Mimameith*, "Mimir's Tree," refers to the Well of Mimir that helps water the World Tree.

Further mystery hangs about the Tree, and there are some details that do survive to the present day. One verse of the Voluspo describes it as an ash tree, but this is one of the few concrete details that survive to the present day. Its roots, according to the Svipdagsmal, are said to burrow into unfathomable depths.[60] It is also unclear when or how the World Tree came into existence. You could interpret this as implying the World Tree has always existed in some form or another, making it a timeless though mutable aspect of the cosmos. This is further emphasized by how the World Tree is one of the few things that will definitely survive the fires of Ragnarök and become the foundation of the world to follow.[61] Surviving sources further emphasize this aura of eldritch grandeur with statements like "few can guess what shall fell the tree," found in close relationship with descriptions of the World Tree and its aspects.[62]

This intriguing combination of supreme importance and puzzling enigmas is a dynamic that defines much of what the World Tree represents in modern practice. Whether your practice leans more secular or mystical, the World Tree reinforces this book's core interpretation of practice that is based on connection, understanding of relationships between different people and Powers, and understanding how their dynamics work as best as possible. For both perspectives, one could argue the World Tree represents an understanding of reality that is founded on a knowable, if mysterious and at times elusive, order. Such a perspective on reality works rather neatly with a more empirical, scientific understanding of existence, as shown by the combination of the World Tree's known role as a sustainer of existence in conjunction with other aspects that remain beyond understanding at this time.

Such associations with order go beyond what is implied by the World Tree's place as the sustainer of all worlds. In the *Prose Edda*, Snorri Sturluson describes

---

60. Bellows, *Poetic Edda*, 242.

61. Rudolf Simek, *Dictionary of Northern Mythology*, trans. Angela Hall (Woodbridge, UK: D. S. Brewer, 2007), 375.

62. Bellows, *Poetic Edda*, 242.

the World Tree as sustained by the Three by drawing water from the Well of Wyrd.[63] A broadly similar process is described in the Voluspo as follows:

Thence come the maidens mighty in wisdom,	Þaðan koma meyjar margs vitandi
Three from the dwelling down 'neath the tree;	þrjár, ór þeim sal er und þolli stendr;
Urth is one named, Verthandi the next,—	Urð hétu eina, aðra Verðandi,
On the wood they scored, —and Skuld the third.	skáru á skíði, Skuld ina þriðju;
Laws they made there, and life allotted	þær lög lögðu, þær líf kuru
To the sons of men, and set their fates.[64]	alda börnum, örlög seggja[65]

This process is what helps define the broader ørlog of all of reality. These scorings shape the conditions that influence beings in all worlds, including ours.

The regular use of the Old Norse word for law, *log*, to describe what was imbued into humanity reveals even more about the place of the World Tree in the cosmos. *Ørlog* bears a close linguistic relationship with *log*. Many have interpreted this connection to treat ørlog as something approximating a cosmic form of law, and there is something to this approach when you unpack the Nordic concept of how law worked and was made. Laws, both before and after conversion to a limited extent, were a product of mass popular Thing (pronounced "ting") assemblies that met in open-air spaces to adjudicate disputes, set policy, and pass new laws. These laws were then enforced by the whole of the community instead of by any specialized, professional body set aside to handle crime

---

63. Sturluson, *Prose Edda*, Gylfaginning 16.

64. Bellows, *Poetic Edda*, Voluspo 20.

65. "Konungsbók eddukvæða GKS 2365 4to," Stofnun Árna Magnússonar, accessed December 16, 2022, https://www.arnastofnun.is/is/konungsbok-eddukvaeda-gks-2365-4to.

and punishment. While this system certainly wasn't a perfect image of modern egalitarian ideals or justice, with enslaved people possessing significantly fewer rights before these bodies than free members of society, the Things did represent a rough sort of direct democracy. Laws, broadly speaking, were made and maintained by the people who were bound by them.[66]

This system's influence is clearly manifest in surviving mythic materials. According to Snorri Sturluson, the gods are said to hold their assemblies at the foot of this great tree and lay down the laws that bind all present to agreed-on courses of action.[67] Other references to godly assemblies in the Voluspo, particularly during the creation of Midgard and in the days leading up to Ragnarök, strongly suggest this motif of gods resolving their disputes in a similar fashion to what was employed by humanity on Earth has some basis to it, even though there is no reference in the Voluspo to where these assemblies took place.[68] If these assemblies could be seen as following a similar pattern to those in Midgard, complete with taking place in a neutral, open-air space, then Sturluson's assertion of the World Tree's status has at least some basis in an extant tradition or interpretation that existed in regional folklore and myth. Accepting this element into practice further reinforces the World Tree's status as a neutral, crossroads space outside the Nine Worlds where questions of cosmic order are resolved, complete with the Norns, whose work sustaining the World Tree keeps this world of law moving.[69]

It is, therefore, fully justified for modern practitioners to treat the World Tree as both the core of the cosmos and a broader metaphor for the organic, evolving orders that emerge in healthy ecosystems. The World Tree also fits neatly as a beautiful representation for fundamental forces like gravity and magnetism, complete with the continuous struggle against Nidhoggr's gnawing entropic decay. This same metaphor of support systems that are essential for existence can also extend to ecosystems, habitats, and societies with equal

---

66. Gwyn Jones, *A History of the Vikings* (Oxford, UK: Oxford University Press, 1984), 50–51, 92–93.

67. Sturluson, *Prose Edda*, Gylfaginning 15.

68. Bellow, *Poetic Edda*, Voluspo 6, 9, 24, 25, 48.

69. Else Roesdahl, *The Vikings* (London: Penguin Books, 2016), 59, 61; Jones, *A History of the Vikings*, 50–51, 92–93; Robert Ferguson, *The Vikings: A History* (New York: Penguin Books, 2009), 164–165.

ease. Regardless of the specific application or interpretation, the World Tree's properties, influence, and significance make it an effective framework for understanding the systems of interdependence necessary for making life and society possible. It is truly fitting that the best possible representation of the cosmos would be a vast, mysterious tree.

The Nine Realms of the World Tree

Regardless of your specific practice and relationship with the Otherworlds, these Nine Realms are critical elements of the cosmos. All are places where much of the action in the mythic sagas unfolds and vast domains that represent critical concepts in modern Nordic-derived practices. Each of these layers of the cosmos is as vast as Midgard, filled with beings of all kinds, including those that each realm is most famous for. Understanding what the Nine Worlds represent, both in context and for the practitioner, can bring new insights and help strengthen relationships with the Powers who dwell in these places.

There are many ways you could explain how the Nine Worlds relate to physical reality as we know it. In Fire and Ice practice, there is no single, definitive answer to what these Otherworlds are. Though Snorri Sturluson vaguely refers to realms such as Jötunheim as being located "in the East" and claims the Aesir originally came from Asia, specifically Troy after the end of the *Iliad*, there is nothing that definitively answers if the ancients saw these realms as distant locations on Earth or truly otherworldly places.[70] All of this is further muddied by claims made by Sturluson in the Heimskringla that many of the gods, including Odin and Freyr, were ancient kings who became worshiped as gods.[71] These points could be used to argue that the ancients viewed the Nine Realms as literal, physical places that lay beyond their knowledge, making them effectively otherwordly.[72]

Standing in contrast with this possibility are elements present in the lore that suggest a different understanding. This begins with how the Realms are described. Midgard is described as a vast realm that is fenced off by the eyelashes

---

70. Sturluson, *Prose Edda*, Gylfaginning 2–3.

71. Snorri Sturluson, *The Heimskringla*, trans. Samuel Laing (n.p.: Andesite Press, 2015), Ynglinga Saga 2–14.

72. Sturluson, *Prose Edda*, Prologue 2–5.

of Ymir and the vast bulk of Jörmungandr resting beneath an impassable ocean, suggesting an understanding of a reality that stretched beyond the world as they knew it. Asgard, similarly, is girthed by a great wall and is only suggested to be connected to these other realms by means of the Bifrost Bridge, whose foretold shattering in Ragnarök reinforces the sheer vastness of the armies of Muspelheim.

What further separates Asgard, and by extension the other Nine Realms, as distinct places unto themselves is how the only other reliable means of trans-portation between realms are equally extraordinary and uncommon. Aside from Sleipnir, Odin's eight-legged horse and son of Loki, and Freyr's magic folding ship, there are few references to any Powers traveling easily or freely between the Realms. The one exception to this is Sturluson's depiction of godly assemblies being held at the base of the World Tree, which further enforces how significant the World Tree is to this cosmic order.[73] All of this strongly suggests places such as Asgard and Vanaheim were not seen as existing off in distant Asia or another, undiscovered country but as different realms that exist according to their own rules and can only be reached using very specific, un-usual means.

A more modern interpretation, based on the latter of the two possibilities, takes an even more sweeping view, building heavily on a more otherwordly interpretation of the lore. What is described in these examples of surviving source materials is a record of human beings trying to understand powers and forces that, when taken at face value, are genuinely beyond human comprehen-sion. It, therefore, follows that what is known of their realms are only fragments of an already limited, filtered perspective on aspects of reality that operate on fundamentally different rules. In this view, the Nine Realms are seen as different layers of reality or alternate worlds, as posited by multiverse theory, which play host to different kinds of entities and forms of existence. This perspective, fur-thermore, does not rule out the possibility of other divinely associated realms, as it is certainly possible there are far more than nine realms on the World Tree.

Whether taken as metaphysically true or rich metaphor, the core of this view sees the Nine Realms as frames for understanding critical aspects of the human experience and the world around us with immeasurable depth and countless

---

73. Sturluson, *Prose Edda*, Gylfaginning 15.

mysteries waiting to be explored. The descriptions of these realms that follow are drawn equally from the lore, from experiences during trance journeywork, and from their inhabitants' most common associations.

Midgard

The best place to begin when discussing the Nine Worlds is Midgard, the realm everyone is most familiar with. Its name is translated to mean the "Middle Place" or the "Middle Realm," and it is often seen as being anchored halfway between the World Tree's roots and upper canopy. Midgard is the creation of all the Gods and was fashioned from the body of the primordial frost giant Ymir. The Voluspo describes this process as follows:

> The sun, the sister of the moon, from the south
> Her right hand cast over heaven's rim;
> No knowledge she had where her home should be,
> The moon knew not what might was his,
> The stars knew not where their stations were.

> Then sought the gods their assembly-seats,
> The holy ones, and council held;
> Names then gave they to noon and twilight,
> Morning they named, and the waning moon,
> Night and evening, the years to number.[74]

This ordering of the heavens is just as essential for understanding Midgard as the shaping of the Earth. These verses imply that Midgard is more than just the third planet in orbit of a star named Sol on the edge of the Milky Way galaxy; instead, it makes up all physical reality as we know it. Everything from Earth's fiery, molten core to the farthest flung objects floating in the great void beyond lies within the bounds of the Middle Realm, all encircled by the Midgard Serpent known as Jörmungandr, which upholds the edges of material reality until Ragnarök.

---

74. Bellows, *Poetic Edda*, Voluspo 5–6.

Jötunheim

Nearest to Midgard is the realm of Jötunheim, the home of the Jötnar. As the abode of the most primal of the godly Powers, Jötunheim could be seen as a place of untamed wildness where the works of humanity are at best rumor and conjecture. There are few sagas set within its borders, and in all cases they follow travelers who enter Jötunheim as part of a greater journey or in pursuit of a particular goal, in the case of Skyrnir's wooing of Gerd on behalf of Freyr. Those who seek to take anything from Jötunheim, whether the hand of a mighty Jötun or even the liberty to leave the realm, comes at cost for the traveler. Those who work with or in Jötunheim must always be aware they are visitors in this wild, untamable place and there is little room for those who do not respect the Jötnar's realm. Jötunheim is often experienced in trance journeywork as the paramount wilderness, a place utterly unmarked by the works of humanity and left wholly to its own devices. It is an utterly elemental and wild place, and all who pass through will find themselves irrevocably changed by their experience.

Niðavellir

Also close to Midgard is Niðavellir, also known as Svartalfheim, the home of the dvergr, who are better known as the dwarves. Where Jötunheim is wild and fierce, Niðavellir is a fastness of the Powers most strongly associated with craft, industry, and creation. These halls are the workshops where the greatest of the Aesir's treasures were crafted by smiths of paramount ingenuity, ranging from Thor's mountain-smashing hammer to Freyja's amber necklace and the slight ribbon crafted from impossible things that binds Fenrir until the Doom of the Powers.

For modern practitioners journeying in this place, do not be surprised if the forges of Niðavellir take on a more industrial, digital, futuristic, or archaic appearance. As the vættir most closely associated with modes of production, craft, and industry, it is only proper for the dvergr to have experimented with many different tools. Even though this would all suggest this is a realm of sterile order, Niðavellir can be just as elemental as Jötunheim. While one represents the endless potential and fecundity of life, the other feeds the fires of transformation and innovation. This world is a place where ideas are realized as possibilities and impossibilities are given tangible forms.

Asgard

Moving up the World Tree brings you to Asgard, the home of the Aesir. It is here that all the gods of humanity keep their halls, raised on the lush, rolling plains they raised from the void that followed Ymir's demise. Asgard is connected to all the Nine Realms through the Bifrost, the Rainbow Bridge watched over by Heimdall, which allows for travel to and from the Aesir's halls to any other place along the World Tree. All the Aesir and the Vanir who they took as hostages following their ancient war can be found in Asgard, along with many of their most prominent allies, including the einherjar warriors of Valhalla. How Asgard appears to practitioners engaging in journeywork varies, though the common tendency is to describe it as idyllic. This makes a certain amount of sense, as Asgard is initially depicted in the Voluspo as something of a paradise:

> At Ithavoll met the mighty gods,
> Shrines and temples they timbered high;
> Forges they set, and they smithied ore,
> Tongs they wrought, and tools they fashioned.
>
> In their dwellings at peace they played at tables,
> Of gold no lack did the gods then know,—
> Till thither came up giant-maids three,
> Huge of might, out of Jotunheim.[75]

This strongly suggests that Asgard was, and to an extent still represents, an ideally abundant environment for a community to thrive in. As Asgard is the home of the gods most closely tied to human affairs, it only stands to reason that our understanding of their domain is one where none lack for what they need and there was peace, if only briefly.

Vanaheim

Alongside Asgard is Vanaheim, the home of most of the Vanir. As the home of the gods of the liminal, it is a place of great mystery and magic. Where the

---

75. Bellows, *Poetic Edda*, Voluspo 7–8.

Aesir were said to be paramount in martial prowess, the Vanir were able to fight them to a standstill thanks to their mystical prowess, a skill that permeates their home. The Vanir's associations with human interactions with nature run strongly through this place, offering the wisdom that comes from moving between worlds and working in concert with many places. Some might describe it as almost fae-like, filled with the logic that comes from such deep knowledge of the liminal and places of transition. Any who would pursue the wisdom of Vanaheim approach a place of great power and majesty, focused on relationship and connections with the rest of reality.

Alfheim

These two realms are further joined by Alfheim, the home of the alfar. These potent Powers are said to have their own mystical potency, an association that is further reinforced by their close connection to the Vanir through Freyr. It is here that these beings associated with hidden knowledge in Midgard, possessing of their own power to grant favor or harm, raise their halls. Even as this is a realm beyond our own, the alfar are not themselves strangers to humanity and are said to dwell under hills and other similar places throughout Midgard. For any seeking to work more deeply with the alfar, Alfheim is a place worth journeying to, provided you carry yourself with the same respect that would be granted to any host. As home to beings who are known for manipulating perception and appearances, it would behoove any traveler to be wary when seeking wisdom here.

Muspelheim

Following Ratatoskr, the gossipy otherworldly squirrel, down the World Tree brings the traveler to the realms tied to the World Tree's base. On one side, one finds the raging inferno of Muspelheim, the land of fire. This was the home of the great flames that rushed in to the Ginnungagap countless ages ago and is said to be where the great Jötun Surtr makes their hall. Muspelheim's endless heat brings with it the promise of rapid transformation and change that comes with fire. Sometimes this can be highly destructive yet still necessary, as many changes in life require great upheaval. Journeying here should not be done lightly, as this is a realm of the same furious intensity that melts steel, burns homes, and ignites stars. Muspelheim is all that fire is, from the flickering candle to forest-consuming infernos and volcanic eruptions.

Niflheim

Opposite Muspelheim is Niflheim, the realm of ice where the surge of frost mixed with flame created the building blocks of reality. One could be tempted to see this as a place of endless, unchanging cold like the preindustrial Arctic or Antarctic regions of the world. This, however, misses how complex and nuanced the Nordic people's understanding of ice was. As is shown in sources such as the Norwegian and Icelandic rune poems, ice was seen as possessing its own transformative power that is expressed most succinctly in the Norwegian rune poem with the line "Ice we call the broad bridge."[76] This is further attested by the discoveries of geologists who argue that hills, valleys, and mountains in some regions of the world, such as the Highlands of Scotland, were the product of thousands of years of patient glacial movements.[77] Niflheim, similarly, embodies this kind of steady, grinding change that leaves all it touches forever transformed. As a deeply primal place, Niflheim is not recommended for the inexperienced or unprepared journeyer, as, much like Muspelheim, it is home to one of the fundamental forces driving the cosmos.

Helheim

The last of the deep realms is Helheim, the home of the dead presided over by the corpse goddess Hel, which is discussed in further detail in chapter 6. Most of those who die in Midgard will find their way here, and it is implied that Helheim plays host to more than just humanity's deceased. Baldr, one of the Aesir, is said to enter Helheim following his demise at the hands of his brother Hodr, suggesting that Hel's Realm is tied deeply to the processes of death for all things, including gods. Helheim is a place of rest from the labors of life as the departed enjoy well-earned relief and this realm is implied, in some places, to be a place without death filled with peace and plenty. As home for the vast

---

76. Bruce Dickens, ed., *Runic and Heroic Poems of the Old Teutonic Peoples* (Cambridge, UK: Cambridge University Press, 1915), 26.

77. "The Ice Age," NatureScot, February 18, 2022, https://www.nature.scot/landforms -and-geology/scotlands-rocks-landforms-and-soils/landforms/ice-age-landforms/ice -age.

majority of Midgard's deceased, Helheim is a good place to start when seeking to commune with the dead. Even if the specific individual you are seeking does not rest on Hel's benches, it is likely they can at least point you in the right direction.

The Three Wells

Also found near the roots of the World Tree are the Three Wells, known as the Well of Urdr, where the Norns draw water for the Tree; the Well of Mimir, where Odin sacrificed his eye for wisdom; and Hvergelmir, where Nidhoggr gnaws at the World Tree's roots when not devouring the most dishonorable of Midgard's dead. These wells provide sustenance to all of reality. The Well of Urdr in particular is the source of all new possibility that is drawn forth by the Norns for imbuing into the World Tree. The Hall of the Three Greater Norns can be found by the shores of this well, though journeyworkers are cautioned against visiting the Three as even the gods are loathe to disturb their work. The Three Wells are a potent place for any sort of journeywork, particularly for those who wish to commune with the greater wyrd. The only well that one should avoid is Hvergelmir, as Nidhoggr's endless hunger makes the ill-omened space particularly dangerous for trance journeyworkers.

The Eagle, the Squirrel, and the Dragon of the World Tree

The last figures worth mentioning are found above the heights of the World Tree. Nested in the peak of the World Tree's cosmic canopy, is a great nameless eagle that has the hawk Veðrfölnir perched on their head. What this eagle does or why they dwell here is a mystery, as is Veðrfölnir's place in the cosmic order. The only thing known for certain is the eagle's nest is one of the two stops for the squirrel Ratatoskr's endless journey: they run from canopy to the deepest roots, spreading rumors from one end of the Nine Realms to the other. Ratatoskr's chattering fuels an endless feud between the eagle and the dragon Nidhoggr in a fashion not unlike many posters of edgy takes on social media.[78] Perhaps this eagle has their own insights into the greater order of reality, though what these are is unknown as, unfortunately, few sources describing them survive.

---

78. Sturluson, *Prose Edda,* Gylfaginning 16.

Beyond the deep realms of the Nine Worlds lies Nidhoggr, the great dragon who endlessly gnaws at the roots of the World Tree. Their hunger is endless, as is their desire to devour, though neither will ever be sated, as the World Tree grows on in spite of their efforts. It is strongly recommended that any seekers steer clear of this beast, for their hunger is endless.

The Ironwood

Another place that is connected closely to Midgard but is not held in the same esteem as the Nine Worlds is the Ironwood. Described as being directly to the far east of Midgard, the Ironwood is the domain of Angrboda, the Troll-Queen and master of seiðwork. Other trolls of exceptional age, wisdom, and prowess are said to dwell within the Ironwood. This place can be seen as a reflection of the primeval forests of ancient Europe that once covered large swathes of Scandinavia, representing a kind of mythic wilderness where anything could happen. Journeyworkers may find the Mother of Monsters and other potent trolls dwelling within the Ironwood, suggesting that caution should be taken when working with this realm.

Moving between Worlds

In Fire and Ice practice, ecstatic journeywork within the Nine Worlds is used as a tool for furthering spiritual and personal knowledge. Though there is no direct evidence that the specific framework for such practices, or the related interpretations of the Nine Worlds, were present in the pre-conversion period, these practices nonetheless plant their roots in related practices that were known to have existed.

In lore and surviving source material, travel between the Nine Worlds is certainly possible, though not common. All the Aesir are at least implied to have the means to enter the other realms through the use of the Bifrost Bridge.[79] Odin himself is said to move freely between the worlds thanks to his eight-legged Sleipnir, an ability that is clearly implied as unusual.[80] There is also some degree of uncertainty regarding the place of Powers like the alfar, who both have their own realm and dwell in Midgard, and whether they can traverse

---

79. Sturluson, *Prose Edda*, Gylfaginning 13.
80. Sturluson, *Prose Edda*, Gylfaginning 42.

these cosmic boundaries. Some völur (seers) are described as having the power to commune with the dead and, in the case of the Greenland völva in Erik the Red's Saga, even become a channel for their words, but how this relates to the boundaries between worlds is left unexplained in the text.[81]

Even though this ability is not common, such journeying can be a source of wisdom. Odin's endless wanderings are implied to be driven by his deep hunger for information, pushing him ever further along the boundaries of known and unknown. Thor, Loki, and Thjalfi's famed journey into the East saw them encounter illusions, challenges, and contests that pushed them to the limits of their strength, appetites, and speed. These themes of gaining wisdom of self and the world echo the journeys undertaken by Nordic seafarers who, seeking wealth, plunder, or even just what lay beyond the horizon, traveled from as far as Baghdad and Newfoundland in pursuit of their goals. Far from promoting insularity and isolation, the lore and history tell tales rooted in going into the unknown and learning from what you encounter.

Utiseta

In Fire and Ice practice, journeywork uses the tools of utiseta to enter a controlled, deep ecstatic state. This is often done using meditative techniques (such as those outlined in this book, at the end of this chapter, and in *The Way of Fire and Ice*), but they can also be achieved with the use of music, dance, ritualized movements such as working a drop spindle, or whatever other tools work best for you. Once the practitioner has reached this state, they project their hugr, often with the assistance of their fylgja, into the Otherworlds and use the World Tree as the path for reaching these realms. From there, it is possible for the practitioner to seek guidance from the beings that live on the World Tree; seek out any one of the Nine Realms; approach the Wells of Mimir, Urdr, and Hvergelmir at the base of the Tree; or otherwise approach anything else that is connected to Yggdrasil. All of this is metaphysically possible thanks to the hugr's and fylgja's documented ability to move freely from their associated form and the World Tree's deep connections with every one of the Nine Worlds. This freedom of movement makes it possible for the Self to reach the

---

81. Sturluson, *Prose Edda*, Gylfaginning 13, 42, 43–47; J. Sephton, trans., *Saga of Erik the Red*, Icelandic Saga Database, chap. 34, https://sagadb.org/eiriks_saga_rauda.en.

Otherworlds, especially with the help of the fylgja, while the branches of the World Tree provide pathways out, into, and between these realms of existence.

For the mystically inclined, utiseta journeywork is an effective tool for obtaining otherwise inaccessible knowledge, communing with the Powers of the Otherworlds, and learning from the beings most closely connected to the World Tree. In the hands of an experienced practitioner, these techniques can be one of the most versatile implements for deepening your spiritual work.

The primary foundation for Fire and Ice journeywork lies in the seiðr practice of utiseta, the art of going under the cloak or sitting out on a grave mound to gain answers and guidance. The most famous documented case of an individual going under the cloak was Iceland lawspeaker Thorgeir Thorkelsson in the year 1000 CE. Facing the impossible dilemma of resolving the sectarian conflict between the pre-Christian inhabitants of the island and the recently converted Christians, Thorgeir sought answers by going apart from the Althing and sitting under his cloak for several hours. There is no description of what he experienced or if he ever shared what occurred during this time, but whatever happened, it led to Thorkelsson's compromise solution, which was accepted as valid by both factions. There is even less internal description of what the Greenland seeress from Erik the Red's saga did to channel the voice of the deceased or what countless others did to commune with the dead interred under earth. Even so, there is a consistent pattern of using deep, ecstatic meditation to obtain information from potentially otherworldly sources.[82]

From a more secular perspective, this practice of journeywork and the questions posed by the greater structure of Radical Heathen cosmology are equally justified, though for different reasons. Journeywork, from this perspective, is a form of self-guided meditation that helps you focus your attention toward specific ideas or archetypes. You could argue that such meditative work has validity because the imagery of the Nine Realms, their inhabitants, and the World Tree are highly useful frameworks for structuring a meditative practice. Their associations in Fire and Ice practice, as discussed in this chapter, make them especially useful for focusing your intentions and engaging with specific questions that you may see as associated with the symbolism of each realm or the Powers dwelling within. The World Tree itself, similarly, can be a highly useful

---

82. Heath, *Elves, Witches & Gods*, 19; Sephton, *Saga of Erik the Red*, chap. 34.

mechanism for exploring your connections with others, society, and the world around you. If the only thing you take away from this form of utiseta journeying is that it can be an evocative set of tools for understanding the world, then that is just as valid as those who argue for more mystically inclined perspectives.

Regardless of your particular take on this practice, there remain some ground rules that need to be discussed before you begin any sustained journeywork. These guidelines are based on the experiences of practitioners, common concerns, and some key factors to consider. Whether you consider this practice to be a form of guided meditation or spiritual travel, all are important to consider before preparing for utiseta journeywork. These concern the potential hazards that can face people engaging in such practices, some critical factors to consider when traveling through the Otherworlds, and some discussion on using hallucinogenic or psychoactive substances as part of your practice.

Related to such preparations is understanding the realms you are seeking to enter as best as possible given limited source material. Even though much of the Nine Worlds, including Midgard, is more mysterious than known to humanity, any information is always more useful than none. Take some time, through study and meditation, to learn more about the Powers you could expect to encounter in the Otherworlds and what they are associated with. You should also, similarly, read up on the realms themselves and their own associations, as these can give some hints about what you can expect in these places. Be sure, when doing such work, to be mindful of the limits of what is generally known and prepare yourself for making a quick exit if it should become necessary.

No matter how much preparation you do, you should always remain open to the potential to be surprised by what you will find in the Otherworlds. These are, after all, realms that range from places of eternal sun-hot flame to abyssal frost, the wild fastness of Jötunheim, and the ultimate crossroads that ties all forms of existence together. Such places, to put it bluntly, do not and will not conform to any Midgard-based expectations you may have for how everything from living beings to the laws of physics are supposed to work. Always be ready for your circumstances to shift dramatically from largely following the laws of physical reality to a sudden plunge down a rabbit hole of shifting landscapes, beings of fire and frost, or other equally surreal happenings. As illogical or dream-like as this work can get, even initially unexplainable events can provide their own wisdom for travelers, though it may take some time to tease out meaning from some of your more enigmatic experiences.

This raises the question of possible risks and traumas. Even though what is happening is not physically taking place, it is still quite possible to enter psychologically and spiritually traumatic situations. You may enter realms or encounter Powers whose actions and behaviors may be deeply psychologically triggering, digging up past harms in uncontrolled and potentially harmful ways. From a more metaphysical standpoint, projecting your hugr into the Otherworlds puts one of the key elements of your Self in a position where it can, potentially, face harm from those who dwell elsewhere on the World Tree, as can your fylgja. These Powers are, after all, not tame animals to be gawked at or reflections of your ego that exist solely to satisfy your desires. Such risks are especially important, as all these realms are, fundamentally, alien to the human experience in many critical ways. No matter where you go or how long you spend time in these realms, you will always be a visitor coming from a profoundly different aspect of reality.

Two practices that can help mitigate such risks are developing your relationships with your fylgja and any other friendly Powers, such as particular vættir, alfar, and gods. Your fylgja is probably the most valuable of these allies thanks to the intimate connection you share with them. As an element of your Self, they have a strongly vested interest in keeping your hugr safe from harm, as any harm done to your hugr will also be felt by your fylgja. There are also, owing to their in-between nature, more familiar with otherworldly spaces than your conscious mind is and can help guide you in unfamiliar conditions. If worse comes to worst, your fylgja's connection with your Self makes it possible to follow your fylgja back to your form, beating a hasty retreat from danger.

Allied Powers can, similarly, be helpful in related ways, though it is important to remember they do have their own needs, desires, and goals. Some of the trickster figures, such as Odin and Loki, may be prone to thrusting you into uncomfortable circumstances, while others may refrain from certain journeys for their own reasons. Conducting journeywork with allied Powers always requires careful negotiations with them, and it is recommended you only bring them in for journeys that you expect will be especially risky or may require their particular expertise. No matter what, always be ready to leave as quickly as possible when you start feeling like you may be in over your head. It is always better to take the prudent course during otherworldly travels and return mostly intact to puzzle out what happened than to suffer serious psychological or spiritual harm.

Understanding these realms, what they represent, and what you can learn from them is a critical component of Fire and Ice Heathenry. Each realm represents distinctly different, critical concepts for explaining the Nordic view of the world and modern Nordic-derived spiritual practices. For Fire and Ice practitioners, this knowledge is especially important for conducting utiseta-based journeywork. The next exercise will help you take your first independent steps into the Otherworlds.

exercise
WANDERING THE NINE WORLDS

This exercise is somewhat like the basic utiseta exercise Going to the Wells from *The Way of Fire and Ice*, also found in appendix I of this book. How Wandering the Nine Worlds differs is this exercise is meant to help you reach the World Tree to journey more freely, whereas Going to the Wells specifically guided you to the wells at the base of the World Tree. Be sure to do any necessary preparation for otherworldly travel before engaging in this exercise.

Begin by finding a safe, relaxing place to sit or lie down and get comfortable. Complete the Understanding the Breath and Calming the Sea and Sky exercises found in appendix I to better get into a controlled ecstatic state.

When you have reached a state of resting calm, begin the World Tree Within exercise found in appendix I. When you feel the connection to the void and the core with energy flowing freely, you may begin the next step.

Call your fylgja to you. If you have not done Meeting Your Fylgja from chapter 3, then please complete that and spend some time with your fylgja before attempting this exercise, as your fylgja is very important for this work. Once you can feel the presence of your fylgja, you may begin the next step.

Visualize the World Tree in whatever form feels most natural to you. When you have an image of it firmly in your mind, reach out your awareness for the first thing in your vicinity that feels directly connected to it. Ask your fylgja to go to where the World Tree intersects with your surroundings.

Ask your fylgja to track this connection back to the World Tree itself. Follow your fylgja as they trace out the trail.

When you have arrived at the World Tree, you will be in a place that stands in connection with all realms. From here, you are free to travel anywhere along the tree or to any of the Nine Realms, including Midgard if you so choose. When you have decided which realm you wish to visit, ask your fylgja to guide you there.

Journey into the realm or place that you seek. When you are ready to return, ask your fylgja to guide you back to your hamr. If you encounter any immediate danger or feel unsafe, you can ask your fylgja to pull you back to your hamr or, in extreme emergencies, use the Three Grounding Breaths to force yourself back into your hamr.

chapter five
A LIVING WORLD

The father of day is Delling called,
And the night was gotten by Nor;
Full moon and old by the gods were fashioned,
To tell the time for men.
—Vafthruthnismol 25, *Poetic Edda*

In modern Nordic practice, everything in the world is humming with consciousness. What holds true in wyrd for all the Powers extends throughout
existence with everything from the smallest microbes to the eldest trees, mightiest whales, and most ancient stellar bodies enjoying a form of immanent sacral
agency. These different entities, beings, and Powers are collectively known as the
vættir, a term often loosely translated as "spirits." Folklore and sagas overflow
with these Powers. They live under many names, such as alfar, dvergr, huldufólk,
tomte, and others that will be discussed more later in this chapter.

Failing to honor these relationships looms equally large, with many stories
of injuries done to the vættir resulting in humans suffering dire consequences.
This complex web of connections makes up what is often described as a Nordic
form of animistic spirituality.

For being such a critical component for understanding this worldview, surviving direct sources from before and during the conversion process produced
from an animistic perspective describing the vættir are scarce, unfortunately.

Fragments have been preserved in the vast treasure trove that is regional folk-lore, but there is little that truly sums up the why of specific experiences, ideas, and practices from the perspective of premodern Nordic animistic practitioners. Even accounts and collections of folklore, as voluminous as they are, suffer from both centuries of drift following the arrival of Christianity and the biases of the antiquarians, scholars, and folklorists who originally catalogued them. This leaves us with some general ideas about what pre-conversion Nordic animism might have looked like, which, unfortunately, lacks many critical details that only a member of that culture could explain and articulate further.[83]

This question of source reliability is of no insignificant concern, as the history of the concept of animism shows. This term is one that has a somewhat loaded history thanks to its origins in nineteenth-century anthropology and religious history. These origins cast a long shadow over the entire concept, as the framing, discourse, and evolution of the term was driven largely by outside observers who frequently carried the additional baggage of the imperial, colonizing powers of the period. For many of these early researchers, animism was seen as a form of backward superstition that was automatically inferior to European Christian societies and a sign of their lack of true civilization.[84] Undergirding such assumptions was the broad-brush application of the term to many different groups in many different parts of the world. This encouraged a tendency to obscure the particulars of the cultures that were jammed together into the box labeled *animism* by unfriendly observers.[85]

Such intellectual and cultural violence justified truly grave acts of physical harm, fueling a cycle of degradation by the often colonial and imperial perpetrators of such destruction that fatally undermined any genuine understanding of such practices. This, thankfully, became increasingly evident as the processes of decolonization began following the collapse of the colonial empires carved out of the Global South and the increasing demands by marginalized groups

---

83. Alda Sigmundsdottir, *The Little Book of the Hidden People: Twenty Stories of Elves from Icelandic Folklore* (Reykjavik: Little Books Publishing, 2015), 17–21; Dubois, *Nordic Religions in the Viking Age*, 30–32; John Lindow, *Trolls: An Unnatural History* (London: Reaktion Books, 2014), 9–13; Nordvig, *Ásatrú for Beginners*, 13–17.

84. Diane Lewis, "Anthropology and Colonialism," *Current Anthropology* 14, no. 5 (December 1973): 581–84, https://www.jstor.org/stable/2741037.

85. Lewis, "Anthropology and Colonialism," 581–84.

in the settler-colonial societies of the Americas, South Africa, and Australia for dignity, recognition, and equal justice under law. Modern anthropology and the study of religion is beginning to undo much of the damage done by their fore-bears, resulting in a new flowering of inquiry thanks to the postcolonial move-ment, yet the damage has clearly been done.[86]

All this said, the best way to shine a new light of understanding for devel-oping modern Heathen animistic practice and what this implies for modern practitioners, Radical or otherwise, was turning to modern Heathens and Nor-dic Pagans for their perspectives on the vættir, Nordic animism, what their ex-istence suggests for how we understand the world, and the many ways these perspectives influence our lives. Emphasizing the lived experiences of contem-porary practitioners further helps emphasize the living relevance of these ideas in motion. These practitioners' responses to my questions through Zoom and emailed interviews, which I'll share throughout the rest of the book, provide further insights on how modern practitioners understand animism, death, and the ways their views on these impact their daily lives.

Dr. Rune Hjarno Rasmussen, Danish scholar of the history of religion and founder of the Nordic Animism group and YouTube channel, shared the fol-lowing about animism: "The word *relation* is my first association. The next are *immanence* and *continuous cosmology*, which is a reality where there is a continu-ity between humanity and other than."

Esteban Sevilla, a Goði for the Asociación Ásatrú Yggdrasil of Costa Rica, offered his view: "I understand animism as the attribution of divinity to nature, even though the general consensus is that plants or other inanimate objects have a soul." Sophia Fate-Changer, the nonbinary Latine Californian founder of the Between the Veils Pagan Convention, said, "Animism must be practices that directly involve working with animals and nature."

A common thread shared by all I spoke with was deep concern for the broader associations of the world and how this has influenced the understanding of the animism concept. Räv Skogsberg, a longtime Swedish Heathen practitioner, said, "I [once] had a more ambivalent feeling about the term, as I connected it to

---

86. Lay Sheng, "A Postcolonial Approach to Social Science?" London School of Econom-ics and Political Science, November 22, 2016, https://blogs.lse.ac.uk/government/2016/11/22/a-postcolonial-approach-to-social-science/.

outdated ideas in history of religion, [such as] the idea of religion evolving from 'simple animism' through the more sophisticated polytheisms to monotheism."

Rasmussen offered a more thorough examination of the origins of these problems:

> When most people hear the word *animism*, they probably have outdated ideas of what it means. You can distinguish their ways of talking about animism into two ways, where one of them is what you see in population surveys. It is also used when people talk about indigenous cultures. [For the first case] a country [like] Nigeria [will be shown to have] a certain segment of Muslims, a certain segment of Christians, and a certain segment of animists. This is a weird kind of label being slammed onto people that have a quite problematic history of colonial baggage.
>
> [The other is when] people project the idea that everything is animate on indigenous groups. This is rooted in the idea that animism is a foundation for more complex or "civilized" forms of religion, and I think this idea [is] incorrect. Contemporary scholarship would say that if you go and you live with animist groups, then you don't find that everything is necessarily animate, and you also find that these realities might have very complex figures such as Nordic gods.
>
> It isn't all this sort of a children's book idea of animism, [where] trees have a soul and the stones have a soul. It can indeed be a bit like that. It can have many different forms and it can take forms such as the pre-Christian Northern European religious practices. That is very much a kind of animism, even though there are these very complex, very composite cosmic deities.

Sevilla offered further elaboration and specifics, rooting his understanding deeply in the natural world: "As a learning environmental scientist, I also see nature and our planet as a whole living organism. To me the gods are an interpretation of this living organism and each of its functions. I can't believe the gods are literal beings, but aspects of nature interpreted by humans."

Fate-Changer had a similar perspective, saying, "I think of it as deeper and advanced works of magic and not just necessarily applying to Nordic mythology or Nordic traditions, but talking about many different types of magical workings globally."

Rasmussen also emphasized that animistic practice may not be as unfamiliar to the modern person as they might think. All these practitioners share a central emphasis on relationship, action, and perspective. Nordic animistic practice is something that is lived by practitioners, not simply accepted as a truism or article of faith. Their practices are all founded to a significant extent on developing relationships with the vættir and the world around us through deeds both great and small, all of which are founded on the core truth that everything in existence is worthy of respect and honor.

Another common thread is how animism is defined by these practitioners as a de-centering of humanity's place in the world. Living things and places have their own needs and concerns that do not revolve around how they are perceived as useful to people but are rooted in the conditions of their own existence. These views gain further depth and understanding when the conversation turns to the question of how we understand the vættir as beings and entities within the Nine Worlds.

Understanding the Vættir

A great place for practitioners looking to deepen their animistic practice to start is by studying the vættir associated with the World Tree and Heathen cosmology. Details on the vættir that survive from the pre-conversion period are somewhat limited, with the alfar and dwarves receiving the most mention of any specific vættr. Further details on these Powers and more information on others come from Norwegian, Swedish, Danish, and Icelandic folklore that was the product of generations of oral tradition. The most significant are alfar (elves), dverger (dwarves), the gnomish nisse and tomte, the more fearsome vittra, trolls, and things that go bump in the night, like huldra, nøkken, and nattmara. Though these sources are not, in and of themselves, products of the pre-Christian past, they nonetheless are derived from peoples who were descended of those groups whose motives for preserving these stories were driven by a desire for fulfilling a need in their communities. There certainly are clear elements of Christian influences, such as the belief that church bells and holy ground repel trolls, but these influences float on the surface of a deep sea of customs, stories, and habits.

Alfar

The alfar, also known as elves, are some of the more diffuse and less well-defined of the vættir. One of their most consistent features is their mastery of magic and illusions, an attribute that is further reinforced by their close ties to the mystically inclined Vanir. Though they are said to have their own realm beyond Midgard, alfar are also described as living in hollow hills and under mounds. Modern Iceland, for example, has many mounds, caves, crevices, and rocks that are said to be inhabited by specific alfar or are otherwise cherished by them. In Sweden, they are said to dance in the mists. This liminal, otherworldly tendency to be present in many different spaces is only fitting for beings so suffused with the boundary-defying prowess at the heart of seiðr.[87]

Dvergr

The dvergr, often referred to as dwarves in English, stand in marked contrast to the more ethereal alfar. If the alfar are defined by their deeply magical natures, then the dvergr are very much aligned with the forces of material production. The dvergr are most strongly associated with craft, forging, and metalwork and are said to dwell under mountains and in the great realm of Niðavellir. Their skills are so great that even the gods depend on them, as shown by famous artifacts like Thor's hammer, Odin's mighty spear, Freyja's Brisingamen, and the great ribbon binding Fenrir in place.[88]

Nisse and Tomte

Nisse and tomte are names for a similar group of gnome-like vættir attested to in southern Swedish, Danish, and Norwegian folklore. They are said to dwell

---

87. Reimund Kvideland and Kenning K. Sehmsdorf, *Scandinavian Folk Belief and Legend* (Minneapolis: University of Minnesota Press, 1988), 45.7–45.8.

88. H. R. Ellis Davidson, *Gods and Myths of Northern Europe* (New York: Penguin, 1984), 40, 42.

on or near specific farms and homes and are often described as small, elderly men not unlike modern gnome dolls. If their inhabitants kept up good relationships with the nisse and tomte through regular offerings of milk and butter, then they would bless their human neighbors with good fortune. Failure to do so, however, would see lands blighted, livestock lost, and crops wither on the vine as the nisse and tomte took their revenge on the homestead.[89]

Husvættir and Vittra

There is great similarity between the husvættir, the spirits of homes, and the nisse, tomte, and vittra, though there is a critical difference. Husvættir are tied more specifically to particular dwellings, while nisse and tomte are associated with specific natural features that are found in spaces inhabited by humans. Similar beings, known as vittra, that are attested to in northern Sweden show similar tendencies and logic as accounts of nisse and tomte, though vittra are often depicted as more distant and potentially hostile. In some cases, whole homes may be relocated if they are believed to be on a vittra-place. Their shared pattern of a place in relationship with humanity shows broad similarity to the nisse and tomte, suggesting they all can be seen as vættir who are often in regular, though not necessarily friendly, contact with humanity.[90]

Trolls

The same could not be said of trolls. These beings, in contrast to nisse, tomte, and vittra, are more strongly associated with wild places distant from human habitation. Folk tales describe trolls living in deep forests, foreboding caves, and on high mountains, though some do wander much closer. Trolls are most associated with ill-happenings and mischief, being seen as disruptive influences that bring their own form of bad luck. Trolls are also strongly associated with great magical prowess, showing some similarity to the alfar. Thor's Hammer is said to repel them, as does the looped troll cross on the next page.[91]

---

89. Kvideland and Sehmsdorf, *Scandinavian Folk Belief and Legend*, 48.1–48.12.

90. Kvideland and Sehmsdorf, *Scandinavian Folk Belief and Legend*, 48.1–48.12.

91. Lindow, *Trolls*, 14–30.

Figure 4. Troll Cross

Huldra and Nøkken

Trolls were not the only vættir dwelling in the wilder places of the world. Huldra and nøkken can also be found when wandering in such places. Huldra are said to dwell in deep forests, playing seductive melodies that can lure unwary travelers to their doom. Nøkken, referred individually as nøkk, live in ponds and other bodies of water. They, like Scottish kelpies, will take on beguiling shapes or the forms of horses that entice travelers to follow them into their watery abodes, where they soon drown. You could see them as manifestations of deep, primal fears that are most present when you are deep in wilder lands, such as getting lost or suffering a terrible fate. They represent the respect that must be given to such places and remind us that even in the present day they still hold their own terrible, dangerous power over our lives if we are not careful.[92]

Nattmara

Nattmara, whose name is related to the English word *nightmare*, are much more intimate. They are said to break into people's homes to ride them ragged in their sleep, leaving their victims exhausted and haggard at daybreak. Sometimes they were said to ride on cattle, draining them of life while in other stories they would appear as gaunt, pale figures who were treated as omens of death. Nattmara could be seen as an ancient society grasping with phenomena like sleep paralysis, though this does not make them any less real as a vættir.[93]

---

92. Kvideland and Sehmsdorf, *Scandinavian Folk Belief and Legend*, 44.1–44.3, 51.1–51.11.

93. Kvideland and Sehmsdorf, *Scandinavian Folk Belief and Legend*, 51.1–51.5.

Valkyries

The eerie otherness is not unique to the nattmara. Surviving descriptions of the Valkyries, fierce Powers of war that some associate with the Norns, show a similar understanding of these more visceral spirits. Valkyries, in later sources and popular culture, are often depicted in popular culture as warrior women stalking the battlefields of the world. Though there are materials that depict the Valkyries in this way, particularly in the Volsungasaga, beneath these examples lies a more visceral foundation rooted heavily in battle.

This pattern begins with their names. Sigrdrifa, the Inciter to Victory; Reginleif, the Power-Trace; and Kara, the Wild, Stormy One, show a consistent pattern of beings who are fundamentally defined by strife. Others are even more direct, such as Hlökk ("Noise"), Göll, ("Tumult"), and Hildr ("Battle").[94] These blunt names are given further shape by the following excerpt from Njal's Saga. It includes an extended, graphic description of a group of Valkyries deciding the fates of fighters locked in battle:

> See! warp is stretched
> For warriors' fall,
> Lo! weft in loom
> 'Tis wet with blood;
> Now fight foreboding,
> 'Neath friends' swift fingers,
> Our grey woof waxeth
> With war's alarms,
> Our warp bloodred,
> Our weft corseblue.
> This woof is y-woven
>
> With entrails of men,
> This warp is hardweighted
> With heads of the slain,
> Spears blood-besprinkled
> For spindles we use,
> Our loom ironbound,
> And arrows our reels;
> With swords for our shuttles
> This war-woof we work;
> So weave we, weird sisters,
> Our war-winning woof.[95]

This visceral imagery of looms weaving the fates of warriors from the entrails of the fallen with swords and arrows as their tools depicts beings whose

---

94. Christie Ward, "Valkyries, Wish-Maidens, and Swan-Maids," Viking Answer Lady, accessed November 1, 2022. http://www.vikinganswerlady.com/valkyrie.shtml.

95. George Webbe Dasent, trans., *The Story of Burnt Njal—From the Icelandic of the Njals Saga* (London: Grant Richards, 1900), chap. 156.

existences are intimately interwoven in the bloody, gruesome work of war. Regardless of how one may perceive or interact with such Powers, these sources make it abundantly clear that the Valkyries were unquestionably seen as beings of battle. This further suggests, as many of the interview respondents observed, that the vættir operate in ways that are ultimately very different from how humanity interacts with reality, and any anthropomorphic depictions are best understood as representations of how practitioners interact with them than a full, complete portrait of any vættr.

These descriptions of the vættir as a vast category of beings with otherworldly desires and intentions in the source material parallel the experiences of modern practitioners. For Dr. Rune Rasmussen, this begins with the sheer diversity and ambiguity surrounding the different groups of vættir. He said, "There is a complex gallery of very different kinds of entities. They have very different properties and personalities. A lot of people who are studying this are really wracking their heads, because scholarship tends to look for clear distinctions, but it is not a given that they were there, that for instance nornir, dísir, alvar could not have been beings with blurry lines between them."

Esteban Sevilla particularly emphasized their strong connections with the natural world from a more ecological perspective, describing the ways that vættir mirror our experiences of natural places. He shared, "In environmental sciences, we see this as the local ecosystem showing its own biodiversity. Each place has a specific set of functions that provide its unique print to the rest of connected ecosystems. The way we interact with the local vættir will affect them inevitably." He further emphasized the extent to which this impacted his understanding of the world and his spirituality. He told me, "To me, the spirit of both biotic and abiotic elements in a given area are unique to each region and are necessary for worship and caring. All of them are necessary for the proper functioning of the world."

Sophia Fate-Changer offered a similar perspective on what could be considered vættir. They said, "The vættir are essentially spirits of the land. Vættir, also known as land wights, can be energies that have always inhabited a place. They can also be spirits of the past, such as animals that have passed on but that have tied themselves to the land. They can be spirits of and energies of indigenous people who lived in those places in the past. They can be anything that's tied to a specific regional location, and it doesn't even have to just be animals. They can be spirits of plants and trees; they can be waterway energies and spirits, even the air currents."

Raven Rissy, Canadian lead singer of the dark electronic folk band Hem Netjer, describes vættir to people who are less experienced with them in this way: "I usually try to explain the vættir in this manner: there are roughly three different kinds: ones that like to be around people, ones that really don't like people, and ones that are indifferent and can go either way. Most people who may encounter the vættir can feel this creepy, spooky, unwanted feeling. That is the vættir who prefer to not interact with humans. That doesn't mean they are evil or bad; they just have a preference and it's not us. There is also the feeling of warmth, comforting, and curiosity from the vættir who do want to get to know us, and that feeling and interaction are worth it."

One particular tendency noted by both Rissy and Rasmussen was the strong, negative reactions from vættir toward people who, for whatever reason, trespassed against them. Rissy said, "I find, in my own practice, some very interesting and often unanticipated interactions with the vættir. It usually happens in moments when you're not ready for it. At times it can be pretty unsettling, but once you realize there is no concept of good and bad, just varying degrees of how much vættir prefer to interact with people, those moments become a lot easier to understand. Some vættir really enjoy the company of humans, some prefer not to [interact], and others are indifferent. It is the ones that prefer to not associate with humans that usually give us that sense of something unsettling." She then further described one case when she felt the vættr of her home was expressing displeasure with the actions of guests in her space. She said, "I felt a difference in my house. It was a very odd experience, and it took me quite a while to bring and welcome back my normal house vættr feeling. I even had a few friends, who knew nothing about the interaction, tell me my house felt different."

Rasmussen stated such experiences and encounters had basis in surviving folklore, providing an example of the general shape and tendencies shown in such stories. He said, "There are examples of a being living in the stone and then the stone is carved into a human shape or is given just a little bit of a human face. Then at some point, the farm is sold to another farmer who's a Christian. He takes a silver bullet, puts it in his rifle, and shoots to kill the spirit. Then all the cows die and the fields grow barren. This story is partly a report of experiences with a wight, but it also has aspects of how to treat the wights well."

These practices are also nowhere near as ancient as you might expect, according to Rasmussen. As he emphasized, "With the home wights, there's been a quite active cult, particularly in Norway, of them continuing far into the modern age."

Cultivating Modern Animistic Practice

Building relationships with such different, even otherworldly, Powers may seem daunting at first. How can one begin to imagine cultivating a relationship with a vast forest, a towering mountain, or an abyssal body of water, especially when source material and the experiences of practitioners show the vættir generally do not behave according to human standards and expectations? The answer to this question is the animistic concept of right relationship. This means developing and sustaining relationships with the Powers around you that are founded on respect for their autonomy, reverence for the places and beings they are associated with, and restoring previously sundered relationships through deliberate action.

Establishing these relationships is a process that takes work, dedication, and shifting how you understand the world around you. Right relationship is more than understanding the specific rituals and practices that are associated with animistic spirituality. It is a matter of living in relationship with the world around you, being mindful of how your actions impact the world, and the ways we all depend on an invisible yet vital web of connections that is responsible for making life possible. In this way, right relationship is life-affirming in the most expansive way possible in how it argues for honoring the dignity and potential of all living beings around you.

These central concepts were clearly expressed in discussions with Esteban Sevilla and Räv Skogsberg. Sevilla was especially eloquent in describing the importance of the vættir in his community's spiritual practice, saying, "We usually worship the land spirits first in each of our blóts. Costa Rica is a place with at least 5 percent of the world's biodiversity, a place where nature surely doesn't sleep. We have consistent weather and longer periods to farm certain crops. Saying this, I can assure that the local wights are usually the most important to us."

As Skogsberg observed, this begins with the smallest of actions and regular ritual, including when holding a blót for the privilege of using the land. He shared, "I also at times give them offerings to help me with growing things in my garden or to guard my house from fire." At the core of both of their experiences is a shared belief in the importance of honoring the beings around us who are essential for making life as we know it possible.

Devotion does not stay confined solely to dedicated ritual spaces and holidays, either in the past or the present. Multiple examples can be found throughout Scandinavian folklore of farmers or others living on the land who maintained relationships with local vættir through regular offerings of common yet valued household items. Milk, butter, and cream were some of the more commonly mentioned items left out on small plates for the Powers to take at their leisure. You could almost see the act of giving up these small offerings to a tomte or alfar as being a part of the daily routine, comparable to washing dishes or doing laundry: a vital, yet relatively mundane task that is necessary for keeping a home livable.

Raven Rissy's personal experiences give some insight into both how these kinds of rituals could be done and the ways you can better understand integrating them into your life.

Rissy explained to me one of her daily rituals for her house spirits and vættir. Every morning she makes Earl Grey tea. Before drinking it, she gives some to a small offering bowl next to her kitchen window. "I find that if you give something that is important to you, it will have more of an impact. I tend to give the first or the last sip as a sign of respect," she said.

The logic of receiving a gift in exchange for a gift holds as true in a working relationship with the vættir as it does in any other case. Incorporating vættir into daily, regular practice is about more than a series of one-way gifts and offerings given to unknowable, local beings. It is a matter of cultivating a sense of mutual respect with the Powers around you that extends both ways.

As your daily practice deepens, you will find your understanding of the wider world shifting to a more thoroughly animistic, engaged perspective that encourages a greater degree of mindfulness for your surroundings. This is both to be expected and part of what is necessary in developing a deeper understanding of right relationship. Cultivating this kind of broader awareness is essential to developing a deeper appreciation for the ways that your actions and choices impact the web of relationships implied by animistic practice. As you deepen your ties with the vættir anywhere, you will soon find yourself developing a similar awareness of your surroundings everywhere you go.

This kind of awareness was a natural result of years of animistic practice for Sophia Fate-Changer. As they described it, "I always try to be aware of where I am, even if it's like a subtle, back-burner awareness. Right now, I am in a hotel in San Francisco on Ohlone land, and because I know San Francisco, I know there's a million pigeons and seagulls everywhere. There are squirrels sometimes and a bunch of raccoons in Golden Gate Park, and I know the kinds of trees and plants in this area. I know that there is obviously big coastal ocean energy here. It's not just a matter of "this is where I am right now." It's where I am anywhere at any time. Awareness that I am on the earth, that I need to be honoring the earth and the beings of the past and the present that are on the earth."

This concern is one that has its own deep roots in Heathen practice and spirituality, specifically in the concept of weregild. Weregild argues that all beings have worth that must be respected no matter how great or small they are. When this is disregarded and harm is done to others, the best course of action under weregild is to make restitution for any damage done and help begin the process of genuine healing. This includes the beings associated with the lands where such harms were done, such as cases of habitat destruction inflicted on the land. Though ritual acknowledgment of these harms does not, alone, begin to make full restitution, it is still a necessary first step for beginning a much larger process of just restoration.

rite
HONORING THE LAND

One particular animistic rite is specifically meant for the purpose of recognizing such harms done to a particular land or place. This rite is distinct from a blót rite and other rites that incorporate ritual offerings for a specific Power in how it emphasizes seeking permission to work with the space rather than assuming a relationship that allows for exchanging of gifts and tokens of support. The spirit of this rite is that of a humble request for permission to begin repairing any damage that has been done. It can, in some cases, be a good starting point for furthering a deeper relationship, though it should not be assumed to always lead to such a dynamic. Some places and Powers have experienced deep harms due to the actions of the past that will take more than recognition of wrongdoing to begin repairing. You should, where possible, use whatever materials or offerings are traditional where you are doing this rite or, if you are unsure, provide something of value, like clean water, freshly prepared or unopened food, or grain.

rite

Begin by introducing yourself to the land using your preferred name and any kennings or bynames you have received from your spiritual community. Ask the land and any beings associated with it for permission to enter their space.

Pour out or place your offering on the land or in a moving body of water, or scatter it to the winds, depending on what you are offering.

Sit in the space for a few moments, taking in everything you can about the environment around you.

Thank the land and proceed based on whatever feels most appropriate. This could, sometimes, mean leaving the space alone due to clear signs to keep out or otherwise respect the space.

Animism on a Burning Earth

These questions of healing, restitution, and right relationship show animistic perspectives cannot and should not remain confined to matters of spirituality and personal conduct. Animism, especially in times of growing climate uncertainty, challenges many of modern life's taken-for-granted assumptions about how we move in the world. Cultivating an animistic understanding of life calls for a very different approach to the natural world, beginning with both the individual and society's relationships with the natural world.

Every interview subject was very direct in stating animism required realigning our values regarding the natural world, beginning with Esteban Sevilla's direct summation: "I see nature worth worshiping and taking care of, as it is what nurtures us and keeps us alive. When I have communion with the gods, I also have communion with nature and myself."

Räv Skogsberg, similarly, argued animism should encourage a way of living that is "one of respect for all of the world around us—both that which we think of as living and that which conventionally isn't seen as such."

Rune Rasmussen described an animistic approach as being a change of pace along with a change of perspective. He said, "I think our modern way of being in the world is hysterically stressed, unkind, selfish, and exploitative. I think the idea that a mound is inhabited by beings or that specific birds are associated with a specific deity expresses a worldview that could inspire a kinder and slower world."

Raven Rissy's understanding was equally rooted in the same kind of slowness and interconnectedness as Rasmussen's: "It allows you to become more connected with the natural [world], especially with elements that we might just walk by and never notice while we are doing our daily muggle activities." She further emphasized the importance of unplugging to better connect with these broader forces. She told me, "Having a way to decompress from the daily work routine and computers makes it easier to stop and remember that we are made from the same elements that our planet is. Respecting and recognizing that connection is important in helping maintain the balance between the mundane and the spiritual worlds."

Equally consistent in the responses from modern practitioners was how animistic values came into direct conflict with many of the values of the society we live in today. Skogsberg clearly articulated how deeply non-animistic perspectives permeate our lives when he said, "We're conditioned with looking at the world in terms of resources, not relationships, because that's what our societies run on. In all honesty, it's what my life runs on. Everything from the food in my fridge and the fridge itself to the new clothes I bought for my son because it made him so happy—all of that is built on looking to the world and seeing resources."

The destruction of relationships with the land is a major loss felt deeply in many ways. Rasmussen said, "That is something that we've all lost. I often get the feeling that Americans think that perhaps if you lived in Isle of Skye and you spoke Gaelic and wore a kilt and that kind of thing, then you probably have a better connection to the land. I don't think that's the case. I think we're all diasporic leftovers from the rupturing influence of modernity and this destruction of human relation to the landscape."

Sophia Fate-Changer views applying such animist views as a way of rebuilding lost connections with the world and investing our lives with new meaning. They said, "Animism has always gone back to our relationship with the weather, agriculture, and animals, especially animals that we eat. I think that in this modern day, when people are less connected to where their food comes from and less connected to the outdoors, it really brings focus back into what it once was."

All of those I talked to strongly suggested that any form of Heathenry that incorporates any kind of animistic component, as Fire and Ice Heathenry does, must wrestle with these dilemmas and questions. Animism is more than just a different belief system; it is a wholly different way of interacting with the world around us. It is deeply rooted in connection and fostering mutually respectful relationships with the world around us, for what it is while also being mindful of the histories of great trauma that have preceded our present moment. All these relationships are further imprinted into the wyrd and the ørlog, which shapes the ranges of possibilities that lie before us all.

Nothing encourages heeding this wisdom and working to repair the damage done like catastrophic climate change. One could reasonably conclude that if building strong, respectful relationships with the natural world is essential to animistic practice, then it makes logical sense to take action to repair those relationships, regardless of whether they are actively doing harm or are unwillingly complicit thanks to the choices forced by modern social systems of participate or starve. This includes making right with the peoples whose lives were uprooted, torn asunder, or even nearly exterminated to make way for the great, hungering maws of greed and endlessly ever-growing profits and supporting those peoples however one can. No one individual may be wholly or even significantly responsible for the shape of the present day's ørlog, but everyone can choose whether they will perpetuate these increasingly destructive strands of wyrd or transform them into something nurturing, just, and equitable.

Such dilemmas, as the experiences of the interviewees and the hastening rate of climate deterioration show, are more than broad moral, metaphysical, and theological imperatives. They are rooted in the unquestionable reality that everything that lives is intimately dependent on perpetuating mutually beneficial conditions for all our growth. Though the modern world, like a spider spinning a fragile web hanging from a tree, has found ways to isolate large parts of itself from any direct connection to the biosphere, such removal has only ex-acerbated how vulnerable we are. If we collectively chose to cut the final strand keeping this precarious design attached to the tree sustaining it, then we may find out very quickly and painfully what happens to an arachnid that has put it-self completely at gravity's mercy. Such an animistic argument may be strongly at odds with narratives of endless, growing accumulation that drive so much of how our highly capitalist societies live, but it has become clear the real way forward lies in repairing, not ravaging, these now highly fraught relationships while we still can.

exercise
LIFTING THE VEIL

This next exercise is intended to help practitioners foster their connec-tions with the vættir around them by shifting their focus to be more receptive to the vættir's presences. Lifting the veil should be done in a safe, secure space so you have time to adjust to any changes in your perception of reality before attempting to do so with any vættir out in the world.

Begin with the Understanding the Breath exercise found in ap-pendix I.

Let your focus wander and allow the distractions of daily life to fill your thoughts for a moment. Allow all the noise of the mun-dane, ordinary, and routine to enter the space around you. As the noise takes shape, feel it taking on the form of a soft fog. Allow this fog to take shape in the space outside of your mind. If there is a particular visual, such as mist or fog leaking out from your eyes and ears, that helps you see these distractions leave you, feel free to add it in.

Find a space in this fog where it feels thinnest and focus on it. Reach out to this space.

Grab this space and use it to part the fog like a curtain. As the curtain of fog parts, watch and feel it dissipate.

Focus on how this new, unveiled state feels and how it is distinct from the thrum of day-to-day life.

When you are ready to return to your regular focus and perceptions, begin by focusing on your physical form. Take in one deep breath, feeling the ends of your fingers and toes, followed by a second deep breath, focusing on the end of your nose and ears, before finally taking a third deep breath and opening your eyes as you exhale.

chapter six
UNDER THE MOUND

Thou wast, Brynhild, Buthli's daughter
For the worst of evils born in the world;
To death thou hast given Gjuki's children
And laid their lofty house full low.
—Helreith Brynhildar 4, *Poetic Edda*

Death and dying is an area that every form of spirituality has some sort of answer for, and modern Heathenry is no exception. As is fitting for a form of spirituality that is strongly rooted in connection, building relationships, and respecting the sanctity of all beings, death and what is associated with it are viewed in their own unique fashion. In much of Heathenry and especially in Radical practice, death is treated as a transition between different ways of existing in the world. There is no firm note of finality, judgment, or other common associations with death, dying, and passage into what lies beyond. Heathen attitudes, practices, and ideas on death and what awaits beyond are very different from much of mainstream society's.

Continuous cosmology is especially essential for understanding how death and dying are approached in modern Heathen and Fire and Ice practice. This logic of a series of worlds that share deep, abiding connections extends not just to deities and animistic entities. It includes those who have once lived, enfolding those in the grave into a truly expansive understanding of existence. In this framework, death is treated much more positively and less as a singular, defining moment of ending. As both the source material and the observations of interview participants will show, the dead are still very much with us spiritually, and the impact of their actions reverberates long after they have passed on.

Abodes of the Deceased

For the ancient Nordic peoples, the realms of the dead were as varied as the ways the deceased left the land of the living. This is essential for understanding the Nordic afterlife, as it stands in stark contrast to many other, more commonly known understandings of death and dying. For many modern people, the afterlife is seen as a form of reward and punishment. Whether the example is the Christian dichotomy of heaven and hell; the Hellenic realms of Tartarus, the Elysian Fields, and the River of Lethe; or the weighing of hearts from the Egyptian Book of Going Forth by Day, the common theme of judgment is regularly emphasized thanks in part to the heavy influence of prevailing Christian assumptions.

These prevailing views of afterlife as a place of judgment also creep into how people understand the Nordic afterlife. Many less contemporary pop cultural works on death reflect this in some way or another, treating Valhalla as a warrior's paradise and Hel as a place for less worthy demises. This conclusion rests on the broader treatment of the Nordic as a fierce warrior people who lived for glory and destruction and dates to the nineteenth century. This archetype looms large in the popular imagination. It, therefore, makes sense that many assume this pattern was also true for the Nordic peoples and to simply alter the particulars to fit with their romanticized image.

A closer inspection of the available material quickly dispels any notion of the Nordic afterlife as even remotely conforming to such an understanding of mortality. What defines the Nordic abodes of the dead is how those who dwell within left their previous lives. In Radical Heathen practice, specific moral judgments or declarations of faith are not tied to how the dead are treated in the Otherworlds. In Fire and Ice practice, death and its processes are as much an inalienable part of the broader logic of the Nine Worlds as the existence of Wyrd. Certain gods play roles in some of these halls, but these are exceptions rather than the rule. This is all further complicated by the seemingly contradictory fate of the dead in the mounds and tales of the draugr (pronounced *drou-ger*), the restless dead of Nordic myth who are often depicted in the sagas as animated corpses who could also be seen as ghosts by modern practitioners.

The best place to begin is with the known realms of the dead. In modern Nordic spirituality, there are many different places where the departed reside. The most common place for the dead is Helheim, a realm shrouded in mist presided over by Hel, the Corpse-Goddess of the Dead, and is protected by the great wolf Garmr. Hel's Hall was the place of the straw death, for those who died in their homes of old age, sickness, or injury. It is largely treated as a place of rest for the deceased where most could expect to end up, following their ultimate demise.[96]

This understanding of Helheim is clearly influenced by the conditions facing the Nordic peoples. In a time when infant mortality was likely quite high, starvation a very real danger for even the wealthiest members of society, and disease a sufficiently significant problem that the Nordic peoples developed their own quarantine customs well before the outset of the Viking Age, it is rather understandable that Hel's gates would stand open so widely. For most of the Nordic peoples, a straw death was the most likely end they would meet. Going Hel-way carried no particular shame or stigma since it was the fate that awaits most of the living.[97]

In Radical practice, Helheim is a sanctuary for the deceased. It is treated as a place of peace and respite from the labors of life. Many seiðworkers travel to Helheim to seek the counsel of the dead and to offer their guidance to the living. For many Heathens, Helheim is a place of rest for the departed, where most of us will likely meet again one day as part of a greater community of the dead. It is a haven that will even endure the fires of Ragnarök and survive into the new world after.

The broadness of Helheim's hall and any lack of stigma begs the question of whether the warrior's paradise of Valhalla is all it appears to be. The Hall of the Slain is described in the sagas as an impossibly vast place with room for an enormous army. Valhalla on Iðavoll is said to be the place where all who die on the battlefield will awake, having been sent to this place by the will of

---

96. H. R. Ellis Davidson, *The Road to Hel: A Study of the Conception of the Dead in Old Norse Literature* (New York: Greenwood Press, 1968), 74–75.

97. Davidson, *The Road to Hel*, 75–76.

the Valkyries. Now known as the einherjar, they are said to spend their days training for war with all their injuries miraculously healed at sundown.[98] Their bouts are followed by nights spent feasting on the ever-renewing flesh of the boar Særimnir and drinking the endless mead produced by the goat Heiðrun.[99] It is easy to see how this could be seen as a paradise desired by all the ancients even though the source material does not treat it as more or less desirable than any other abode.

As alluring as Valhalla might be for some, there is significant evidence arguing the Hall of Shields, as it is also known, is not simply a reward in contrast to other lesser fates. Valhalla's purpose is to house the warriors who will fight alongside the Aesir at Ragnarök. All who are chosen spend eternity preparing to fight and die one last time in the cataclysmic clash that will usher in a new world to follow. Their new purpose is to set aside any possibility of rest or relief to instead prepare endlessly for a fight they know cannot be won but must be fought.

Valhalla is also not the destination for all war dead. Freyja, the Queen of the Valkyries, receives the first choice of all who are taken by these spirits of war before Odin then takes the remainder to Valhalla. Freyja's chosen dwell in her hall of Sessrumnir on the field of Folkvangr, and their ultimate fate afterward is uncertain. Many theories exist explaining why Freyja is gathering her own otherworldly host, especially since Freyja is not named as one of the Gods who will fall in Ragnarök. Either way, the fact that Freyja receives the first pick of the slain further reinforces that Valhalla's dwellers reach their destination because of the manner of their deaths and not as some kind of special reward.[100]

This consistent theme of the realms of the dead being defined by a person's demise is further evident in the case of Aegir and Ran's Hall. All those who die at sea or by drowning are said to slip beneath the waves to live on in the watery abode of these mighty Jötnar. This idea was so firmly rooted that one expression for drowning was to be caught in Ran's nets. Like Helheim, there is no particular stigma attached to the sea-dead's fate, and seeing as Aegir and Ran's

---

98. Shippey, *Laughing Shall I Die*, 25–26.

99. Davidson, *The Road to Hel*, 66.

100. Davidson, *The Road to Hel*, 66.

Hall is celebrated for the hospitality offered to all the gods, it does not seem to be an unpleasant afterlife in comparison to the other options.[101]

Though these halls are where most of the Nordic dead could expect to be found, they are still not all of what awaits the departed after leaving the world of the living. Further complicating matters is a pair of verses in the Harbard-sljoth, where Thor trades words with the ferryman Harbard, a figure many interpret as Odin in disguise:

Harbarth spake:
"In Valland I was, and wars I raised,
Princes I angered, and peace brought never;
The noble who fall in the fight hath Othin,
And Thor hath the race of thralls."

Thor spake:
"Unequal of men wouldst thou give to the gods,
If might too much thou shouldst have."[102]

This raises further questions about how extensive the Nordic concept of the afterlife is. The argument between Thor and Harbard over the taking of thralls and nobles after death implies divine favor may play some role in where the dead go after their demise. This could be seen as directly contradicting the earlier pattern of deathly halls defined by the manner of one's passing, yet perhaps this reflects a belief that existed parallel to these larger patterns.

It is certainly possible that some individuals who are especially favored by certain gods, for whatever reason, may find themselves welcomed into their dwellings in Asgard, Vanaheim, or Jötunheim after their demise. This concept may have also been a later development in reaction to the coming of Christianity. Either way, the full truth may never be known. For modern practitioners, receiving such favor may be a comforting thought, though it is no better or worse than any other afterlife one might receive.

There is also one further possibility, one that could be seen as paralleling other concepts of the afterlife as a place of reward and punishment. It is said in

---

101. Davidson, *The Road to Hel*, 75–77.

102. Bellows, *Poetic Edda*, Harbarthsljoth 24–25.

some places the most ill-favored of all, specifically those guilty of the crimes of oath-breaking, murder, and kinslaying, would find themselves left wandering at the roots of the World Tree by the Well of Hvergelmir. There they would be set upon and devoured by the great dragon Nidhoggr, the Corpse Grinder, as repayment for their deeds in life as described in the following verse:

> I saw there wading through rivers wild
> Treacherous men and murderers too,
> And workers of ill with the wives of men;
> There Nithhogg sucked the blood of the slain,
> And the wolf tore men; would you know yet more?[103]

Of all possible afterlives, this is the only one that is clearly shown as a negative in the available source material. What is further intriguing is the lack of any indication of this being a result of a verdict cast or judgment rendered by a specific figure. Whether the most heinous of deeds are punished due to reasons deeply embedded in the wyrd of the Nine Worlds, as a direct consequence of the other dead refusing to grant shelter or space to these individuals, or due to another reason is unclear and certainly a topic for rich speculation and argument.

If much of the experiences of the Nordic dead are shaped by how they die, then this possibility raises important questions, particularly how a fate that can clearly be read as punishment could await at least some of the deceased. Some may even go so far as to draw parallels to the Christian hell, a place of eternal torment and judgment, and ask if perhaps it may be a bit hasty to discard any such comparisons. Yet what makes this case more complicated is there is no indication that any particular entity is responsible for assigning this fate to the deceased. If the weight of one's deeds and the causes of death are critical in shaping a person's fate post-mortem, then it is possible those who feed the great dragon are there because of their deeds and their deeds alone.

There are also countless accounts of the dead within the mounds who remain in their burial sites, eternally feasting beneath the earth. In some tales, heroes must break into these tombs to acquire ancient treasures or mythical weapons and confront the re-animated dead who wish to keep their possessions. Some of

---

103. Bellows, *Poetic Edda*, Voluspo 39.

the dead, known as draugr, were said to stalk the lands near their burial for reasons ranging from vengeance against the living to being interred improperly after death and tomb robbers despoiling their post-mortem abodes.[104]

Clearly death and what awaits the deceased in Nordic-derived practice is a very complex subject. Far from being a simple matter of reward and punishment for the faithful, the afterlife is a multifaceted aspect of reality that is defined as much by your wyrd as it is by how you leave the world of the living. For many, the Nordic afterlife is a place of rest from the labors of life spent in the company of the ancestors. Some, such as the battlefield dead, receive a new part to play while others may potentially spend eternity in the hall of a particular god. Only the most horrible in life receive any sort of punishment in death and always for terrible deeds done in life. With the exception of feeding the Corpse Grinder, all aspects of the Nordic afterlife are no more or less desirable, and all are shaped by how you lived and passed on.

Regardless of the hall one enters after dying, what is consistent in all extant sources and modern practice is that death is a change of state. It does not represent a cessation of existence or being sent to face ultimate judgment but is simply a transition from one state of being to another. This does not mean death should be sought in and of itself, as life is still precious and should be lived as fully as possible. As it says in the Havamal of the *Poetic Edda*,

> It is better to live than to lie a corpse,
> The live man catches the cow;
> I saw flames rise for the rich man's pyre,
> And before his door he lay dead.[105]

Yet this does not, in any way, contradict the broader understanding of death as a natural transition experienced by all beings, from the humblest of living creatures to the mightiest of gods. Though the dead no longer dwell among the living in their original forms, they nonetheless remain with us even after passing on spiritually and in the consequences of their deeds. Death, while not something to be actively sought out, is accepted as a natural part of life.

---

104. Davidson, *The Road to Hel*, 80–83; Bellows, *Poetic Edda*, Voluspo 1, 2, 66.

105. Bellows, *Poetic Edda*, Havamal 70.

rite

HONORING THE DEAD

This next rite is intended to help build this connection with the dead and help process any feelings of grief. You can use this for any dead person, whether you knew them or not, though a stronger personal connection will help greatly in fostering an effective working relationship with the deceased in question. This rite can be used for recognizing important anniversaries associated with the departed, marking the passage of time, or any time that has particular significance. Honoring the dead does not, in any way, guarantee the deceased will respond in any discernable fashion to your entreaties and is best understood as an initial gesture, meant to both help the living process their feelings and help cultivate right relationship with those who have passed on.

rite

Begin by collecting items and images you closely associate with the deceased you are recognizing in this rite. Include a small bit of food or drink, preferably something the deceased enjoyed in life.

Lay out these objects in front of a candle, arranged in whatever manner you feel is most appropriate and feels best.

Whisper the name of the departed over the candle and the items you've collected. Take a moment to reflect on your strongest, most meaningful memories of them.

Say the name of the deceased out loud, light the candle, and offer them the food or drink that you have set aside for them. Share whatever words it is that you want to pass on to them at this time.

After you have finished speaking, sit in silence for as long as feels necessary.

When this time has finished, thank the dead for listening and receiving your words. Put out the candle and leave out the food or drink overnight in open air and a place where pets are unlikely to consume it before disposing of it properly and respectfully the next day.

Heathen Perspectives on Death

An understanding of death, the dead, and the living runs strongly through the responses from each of the interview participants. Esteban Sevilla's response roots his understanding strongly in the broader, cyclical nature of Nordic-inspired cosmology. He shared, "Nordic myths of death usually imply a cycle. We are never dead; we are just different in each version of our own composition. Even the myth of Ragnarök implies that after death there is always life reborn; for one thing to live, another one must die. Life and death are always dependent on the other. The Nordic soul complex also implies this. As our soul is usually a composition of different elements, this means we are not only one single aspect; we are a set of aspects that will separate and disperse again."

For Sophia Fate-Changer, this same general understanding of death as part of a broader cycle embedded in the deeper patterns of reality rings as true as it did for the others, with particular emphasis on viewing mortality as a transition rather than an ending. "It is part of a bigger plan in our fate," they said. "Death for me is just a transition to whatever my next purpose is. I can only talk about death in terms of what I believe for myself. As a polytheist, I believe people go where they believe that they're going to go to when they pass on."

Räv Skogsberg emphasized the uncertainties and contradictions inherent in surviving material and folklore on the topic. He described how sorting these points of tension out were critical to developing his views on death in Heathenry. "The myriad of stories about death in the Eddas and sagas leaves a lot open for interpretation," he said. "I have had few problems incorporating many of my preexisting beliefs about death and afterlife. Indeed, with some seemingly contradictory ideas, such as reincarnation and the existence of ghosts, I have been able to find solutions to those contradictions, like the 'soul' being made up of many parts."

This brought Skogsberg to his understanding of death. He explained, "In the end, though, the stories we tell about death and the afterlife are usually not firsthand accounts. It's guesswork and myth building. It seems reasonable to me that in death I'll be close to the deity that I have been close to most of my life, Freyr. I describe what I think that will be like in terms of coming to a party at his home, because that is what I associate him with. Eventually, I'll go to sleep and then someone else wakes up, so to speak."

Raven Rissy, like Skogsberg, had more uncertainty and hesitation about the question but nonetheless expressed a similar faith in the certainty of the greater cycle inherent in all things. Rissy said, "Death is just us moving on to the next life or reincarnation. It seems like moving on to that spirit realm or the place you go continuing with the ancestors and friends and family and all that. There's all the talk about Hel and her realm where everybody hangs out except maybe select few who might be chosen."

These understandings of death also shaped these modern practicing Heathens' views on life in many ways. Sevilla argued that Heathen interpretations on death did not alone cause a significant shift in his views. He said, "The reason why I looked after heathenry was because it matched my points of view. Ever since I left Christianity, these have been my views."

For Raven Rissy, the Heathen views on death push her to live life more fully. She said, "It really makes you learn to live in the here and the now, not worrying if I am going to do all these things and make sure I get the right outcome that I want before it's my turn to go. It forces you to say that you want to do these things and then to do these things if you stay true to who you are and you're not purposely and intentionally hurting people or yourself. Whatever you do, do what makes you feel happy and what makes you have a fulfilled life."

One especially significant element in all my conversations with modern practitioners was the answer to how any potential afterlife impacts their lives. For many living in largely Christian-dominated societies, the question of the hereafter is constantly present in culture and society. One of the main pitches used by many Evangelical Christians is founded on the ever-present question of "What will happen to you after you die?" with the threat of hellfire invoked to drive would-be believers to Christ. When you consider how significantly different and largely non-judgmental the Heathen views on the afterlife discussed so far are compared to the narrative of salvation in heaven or damnation in hell, it is therefore understandable that a lack of such divine judgment may influence their views.

Sevilla's very ecologically rooted views carried through in his understanding of the hereafter. He said, "To me life is here and now. When I die, I will become nature and nature will become me. I don't worry about an afterlife. What was me will return to earth or space if I am cremated, and my energy will be used by other living beings forever. I will be scattered back in the planet that gave birth to me."

For Skogsberg, any afterlife is a small part of his practice rather than a significant, central element. "My beliefs about the afterlife does affect my practice, though not in daily life," he shared. "I have given offerings when members of my extended family have died, and I keep symbols of some of my grandparents on my home stalli. At Alvablót I remember them, toasting them and giving them food."

Raven Rissy stated that, for her, what mattered most is living in the moment. For Rune Rasmussen, the whole question of afterlife and how it influences animist thinking is directly tied to how modern society understands the person and their relationships with the world around them. He further argued for considering the possibility of the dead transitioning into being part of the land around them, ensuring a continuity of sorts that is different from more Christian-influenced concepts. "I think the whole thing about afterlife is a little bit of a Christian idiosyncrasy," Rasmussen explained, "and to such an extent that in modernity as subjectivities have become more bounded, going toward brittle, the focus on afterlife becomes more important. You often hear modern people say that explanation of death and afterlife is the foundational motivation for having a religion at all. That's absolute [nonsense]. Animist polytheist religions should be about life, not speculating about our individual persistence after death."

These modern perspectives on death show several consistent tendencies. All demonstrate a form of acceptance and positivity regarding death, its role in the cosmos, and the importance of building a good relationship with it. There is also no real fear expressed regarding what may or may not happen to them after they pass on, all based on a shared understanding of death as transition. For all, there was a further shared view that any afterlife was a less significant influence on their morality than the impact their actions would have on the people who follow behind them. This emphasis on duty to the living over pursuing a favored place in the hereafter runs strongly for these practitioners.

Nordic Necromancy

It should come as no surprise that Heathenry has its own forms of mysticism oriented toward working with the dead and contacting the deceased. Like many cultures the world over, the pre-Christian Nordic peoples have a wide range of death-related magic and mysticism present in the lore. Two of the most spectacular examples, the Voluspo and the Baldrs Draumr, are from the *Poetic Edda* and feature Odin in his guise as Wanderer compelling answers from the deceased.

The Voluspo is the more famous of the two, as it contains our best surviving account of the creation of Midgard, the origins of humanity, and the signs of the coming battle of Ragnarök. Framing this story is an act of death-related magic in which Odin compels the Nameless Seeress to rise from her mound and answer his questions. Her dialog suggests that while she may have been forced into giving this testimony, Odin is also bound by the working to hear it to the end. The seeress's repeated challenge, "Would you know more?" to the One-Eyed God carries a certain ritualistic rhythm, forcing Odin to consistently reaffirm his desire to go further down the rabbit hole.

The Baldrs Draumr is less known, partly because of its brevity and vagueness in contrast to Snorri Sturluson's description of the death of Baldr in *The Prose Edda*, and it features similar elements. Odin, like in the Voluspo, rides up to the grave mound of the Nameless Seeress in pursuit of answers. In this case, he is motivated by a recent council of gods where Baldr shared he was haunted by terrible visions in his sleep that left him restless and weary. As he does in the Voluspo, Odin under the name of Vegtam compels the Nameless Seeress to tell him the origins of Baldr's nightmares by magical means:

> Then Othin rode to the eastern door,
> There, he knew well, was the wise-woman's grave;
> Magic he spoke and mighty charms,
> Till spell-bound she rose, and in death she spoke:

> "What is the man, to me unknown,
> That he made me travel the troublous road?
> I was snowed on with snow, and smitten with rain,
> And drench with dew; long was I dead."[106]

---

106. Bellows, *The Poetic Edda*, Baldrs Draumr 4–5.

She then, very unwillingly, gives Odin the answers he demands, detailing the name of Baldr's killer and ultimate avenger before revealing that she knows the spellcaster's identity by piercing Odin's disguise and calling him by name.

Both mythic examples fit well with a magical operation that is described in the Havamal:

> A twelfth I know, if high on a tree
> I see a hanged man swing;
> So do I write and color the runes
> That forth he fares,
> And to me talks.[107]

Using such spellcraft was only one of many ways that Nordic mystics communed with the dead. Descriptions of further practices exist in other source materials. The sagas include references of seiðworkers attributed with the skill of conversing with the dead. Some individuals are even described as sitting out on grave mounds to commune with the dead. The result, regardless of the method used, was otherworldly knowledge provided by the departed within.

One consistent, central practice in all these forms was the necessity of liminal space. This is best demonstrated by the well-attested practice of using grave mounds as focal points for necromantic workings. Grave mounds and other burial sites were, for the Nordic peoples, inherently liminal spaces where it was much easier to reach into the Otherworlds and contact the dead. This does not, however, imply deathwork is only possible in places that are close to death. The descriptions of spaeworkers entering trance states during their rites of communing with the dead suggests altered states of consciousness brought these mystics into a similar state of liminality.

This emphasis on liminality is essential for any practitioner seeking to re-engineer a form of modern seið-based deathwork. Pre-conversion Nordic necromancy consistently showed that liminal spaces and states are essential for communing with the dead. Liminal spaces were usually limited in the source material to consist solely of the grave mounds where the deceased was buried,

---

107. Bellows, *Poetic Edda*, Havamal 158.

communing with doorways made for the dead.[108] Modern practitioners may find that memorials, personal shrines, and other forms of remembrance can provide a direct connection to whoever it is they are honoring. Utiseta is probably the easiest form of seiðr to adapt to deathwork. The exercise at the end of this chapter is a modern adaptation of this particular technique and emphasizes using the liminality of trance to reach the dead.

Utiseta journeywork can also be used to travel down the Nine Worlds to the realm of Helheim, the abode of many of the dead. These techniques could be used on their own or in conjunction with a specific place, such as a cemetery or a memorial, that is strongly associated with the dead. Possessory spae could be used in a similar fashion, though it is highly recommended that you have some experience with the art of spae and utiseta-based deathwork before attempting spae with the dead.

You could also take a leaf from Odin's book and use seið-sorcery to commune with the dead. How you do this depends on how your specific practice works, but, as is the case with utiseta and spae, it is critical to account for the liminality factor. Any death-related modern seiðr workings should incorporate items, places, and other representations of the specific dead or death more broadly. Spell-songs and verses should, similarly, try to invoke the kennings and associations of the grave whether or not it is aimed at a specific grave. Bindrunes are one tool you could incorporate in sorcerous deathwork, with two examples, as follows.

---

108. Marianne Hem Eriksen, "Doors to the Dead: The Power of Doorways and Thresholds in Viking Age Scandinavia," *Archeological Dialogues* 20, no. 2 (2013): 192–93, doi:10.1017/S1380203813000238.

Figure 5. Dead Speaker Bindrune

Figure 6. Close the Grave Bindrune

The Dead Speaker is a bindrune crafted by the author to help facilitate such workings. It is intended to give the dead voices to speak and space to be heard by those present. How they express themselves will vary, and it may be a good idea to incorporate other tools or techniques to reach the departed.

This bindrune cannot compel the dead to speak against their will, and if, for whatever reason, they do not wish to communicate, it is best to respect their autonomy and silence. Though it is certainly possible to do this, as discussed earlier with the examples of Odin and the Nameless Seeress, it is not advisable, as this can be a great way to really piss off the dead you are forcing to speak.

The counterpart to the Dead Speaker is Close the Grave. This bindrune, as the name implies, is meant to help ease the active or unquiet dead back into their abodes, whether those lie in the Otherworld or where their remains were interred. Close the Grave could potentially be used to quiet hostile dead, but this should only be done as a last resort rather than a first impulse. It is always better to first find a way to provide equitable, just restitution for the departed than it is to force them back into the ground.

This raises some important questions on moral guidelines for deathwork. In Fire and Ice practice, autonomy is a core value that reflects deep truths that guide all conscious beings. Respecting autonomy extends to every Power and being, including the deceased. As such, you should always do your best to seek the consent of whatever dead you are working with and not impose your will upon them. If you are confronted with especially hostile and potentially dangerous dead, it may be necessary to act in defense of self and others, but you should always seek the consent of the departed first and foremost. You should also always seek to make restitution however you can if you should find yourself interacting in any possible way with victims of colonization. Quieting the angry dead is always preferable to silencing them, especially in places where such rage has simmered unresolved.

exercise
REACHING INTO THE MOUND

However you choose to develop any death-related mysticism, there is a lot of room to explore and adapt for modern practitioners. The next exercise is a specific application of these practices and is based on the ideas discussed earlier in this chapter. It provides you with the tools to use utiseta for communing with the deceased. You should have some regular experience with utiseta practice before attempting this exercise. First-time and less experienced practitioners should not seek contact with any dead who may have inflicted great trauma on you while they were alive.

The purpose of this exercise is to build on Lifting the Veil and to help the practitioner work with the dead. This method works best when in the presence of the grave of the deceased in whatever form that takes or if you have a possession or original likeness, such as a photograph or painting, of the dead you are reaching out to. If you are in a space that you believe is haunted, then it is possible to do this work without either of these elements, as the dead in question is already present.

If the dead you are seeking to contact is someone who was close to you, it is also recommended that you wait at least a year before attempting to reach them, both so they have time to adjust to their new state and to give time to mourn them before engaging in what could be a highly traumatic experience. Please also do not try to use this method for negotiating with a hostile haunting. That is best handled by experienced seiðworkers after eliminating all other possible explanations or possible causes.

Begin with the Lifting the Veil exercise as described earlier in chapter 5.

When your perceptions have shifted, focus your attention on the deceased you are seeking to contact. Visualize everything you know about their appearance, what they did in life, and any names they were known by, including bynames, nicknames, titles, or kennings.

Give time for the dead to take shape. How they appear varies from person to person: some might experience the dead's presence as a particular smell or feeling, while others might see full-bodied apparitions or hear spectral voices.

Once the dead has taken form, you may ask them whatever questions you may have. Remember the dead person is still an autonomous being with its own desires, goals, and history. They are under no obligation to be truthful and might lie or be evasive in some cases.

When you are finished conversing with the dead, make sure to thank them for their time and attention. Visualize them returning to their place of rest.

Shift your attention back to your physical form. Take in one deep breath, feeling the ends of your fingers and toes, followed by a second deep breath, focusing on the end of your nose and ears, before finally doing a third deep breath and opening your eyes as you exhale.

chapter seven
CYCLES OF CREATION AND DESTRUCTION

Out of Ymir's flesh was fashioned the earth,
And the mountains were made of his bones;
The sky from the frost-cold giant's skull,
And the ocean out of his blood.
—Vafthruthnismol 21, *Poetic Edda*

As has been shown so far in this book, change, death, and connection are central constants in understanding the Radical Heathen worldview. These thundering rhythms ripple across the cosmos, fundamentally defining possibility for all beings. All trace their origins in the greater cosmic cycles of creation and destruction, as shown by the Meeting of Fire and Ice, the Slaying of Ymir, and Ragnarök. Cataclysmic transformations of the order of the Nine Worlds reshaped the possibilities of existence for all beings. Even the existence of Nine Worlds on the World Tree is itself a cosmologically recent development that is only first attested following the creation of Midgard.

From root to highest branch, everything on the World Tree is in a state of constant change, growth, and development. These core forces of change, death, and connection are constantly at work through wyrd, and they represent the only truly eternal metaphysical constants in Heathen spirituality. Everything from the smallest of living beings and bits of cosmic dust to the mightiest of Powers, including the World Tree, are subject to these forces without exception. Gods change as worlds are born and ultimately die in a cosmos driven ever onward in a dance as old as material existence.

The most dramatic examples of these forces in action are the reality-transforming clashes that provide the most climactic moments in the sagas. Each of the grand, cosmic events listed earlier are some of the most well-known of the Nordic sagas, with Ragnarök especially celebrated in modern popular culture in every possible medium. There is no denying there is an epic grandeur to each of these world-shaping moments. Each has stakes no less than the ultimate shape of reality, as the struggles of vast entities transformed the foundations of life. Mighty forces embodied as sky-swallowing wolves, globe-encircling serpents, armies of unquiet dead, world-immolating swords, and wizened gods wrestle to define the shape of existence for all beings. It is only fitting that a cosmology defined by its malleability is itself a product of great change, upheaval, and the constant dialectic of creation.

Hand in hand with these consistent moments of spectacular destruction is the promise of renewed creation. These are periods when survivors forge the new from the bones of the old or otherwise take something that already exists and craft it into a totally new form. Nothing emerges from nothing, and everything's origins can be traced to prior, discernible material and social conditions. In the sagas, this begins with Ymir's emergence from a land of frost made by the meeting of Fire and Ice in ancient, primordial times and repeats when the gods use Ymir's body to make Midgard. The same is true when the gods use two trees, Ash and Elm, bereft of all life as the base materials for creating the first humans. Ash and Elm are, themselves, transformed by the three gifts of thought, breath, and warmth, which reshape their ability to interact with the world around them. These reconfigurations of what currently exists into newer forms reinforces how endlessly changeable everything in the Nine Worlds is in Radical practice. What exists is a product of actions and can be altered, replaced, or even transformed by further deeds.

The processes of sacrifice and re-creation are just as present in the actions of the gods as they are in Odin's many sacrifices, ranging from the loss of his eye to offering up himself to himself for nine days and nights on the World Tree, are all products of the Many-Named God undergoing intense, personal transformations to attain greater knowledge of the Nine Worlds. Tyr's giving of his hand to Fenrir shows a similar quality of a significant change fundamentally altering all participants. Freyja's winning of the Brisingamen necklace through her time spent with the dwarves and Freyr's sacrifice of his magic sword to win the hand of Gerd stand as further examples of great transformation brought on through deliberate personal sacrifice.

One final element all things are subject to, as shown in these examples, is an ultimate demise. In modern Nordic Pagan practice, everything from the smallest living beings to the mightiest of gods can and will someday die. Nothing, not even the order of the universe, is truly eternal, with the possible exceptions of the World Tree and wyrd, yet even Yggdrasil will burn in the fires of Ragnarök. This does not, however, carry any implication that existence is pointless or insignificant. If anything, that all things are fashioned from what came before shows every life has a profound impact on the ørlog of all things. Far from implying a grim, potentially nihilistic understanding of reality, the near-total universality of death makes it a shared, transformative experience that clears the way for new possibility.

All these core patterns and cycles derived from them are universal to all aspects of the Radical interpretation of Nordic sagas and modern practice. Like gravity or magnetism, change, connection, and death permeate the Nine Worlds and the lives of all beings within. Everything from the Meeting of Fire and Ice to the winning of the runes and the creation of the first humans follow these deep, abiding forms of reasoning. This, then, begs the question of what this implies for people living in the present day. What does it suggest for our lives when everything is viewed as finite and changeable with no truly eternal constants? Answering this requires more fully understanding how these forces manifest in the lore and the conditions facing the pre-Christian Nordic peoples before then grappling with what this means for the world we live in today.

Song of All Worlds

Those grappling with the questions of creation and destruction would best begin by exploring similar processes throughout the material world. Whether you view the cycles of the World Tree as a deep, resonant pattern that pervades all the cosmos, how the Nordic peoples understood the world around them, or a combination of the two, such investigations of the broader world around you shed further light on the mechanics of existence. What follows is an example of such a frame of analysis, and while there is significant conjecture and speculation, it is nonetheless based heavily on surviving materials that make up the foundation of the sagas on the material conditions facing the inhabitants of early medieval Scandinavia.

One of the best places to start is in the natural world. Environment and climate had profound impacts on the lives of the peoples of the region, many of whom were living in the highly marginal conditions. Winters were a long, increasingly dark time that carried bitter cold, ferocious storms, and plant and animal life entering a phase of long retreat in preparation for lean, hungry times. These were days for drawing in the last harvests, preparing food for preservation, hauling in ships to keep them safe from sea ice, and laying down fuel for fires. Summers, in stark contrast, were long and lush and at the height of Midsummer saw days when the sun never set. In contrast to the forced withdrawal imposed by winter, summer was a time of warmth, growth, and boundless potential. Crops were planted, ships sailed on calm and ice-free seas, and communities flourished. Yet even this comparative bounty was beset with uncertainty. Summer storms could wreak havoc on the best laid ventures whether on land or sea, and the warmer months also enjoyed the dubious honor of being the prime season for warfare. Life was driven by this cycle of heat and cold, all balanced above the ever-present risks of hunger, injury, and illness.[109]

These stark realities were reinforced by the very nature of the environments themselves. Unlike other parts of the continent, the Scandinavian peninsula and its neighboring islands were far from optimal regions for developing settled, agricultural societies. Much of the modern Norwegian coast consisted of small, glacier-carved valleys flanked by towering mountains. The neighboring flatlands of present-day Sweden were more hospitable, but much of the lands beyond coastal regions or riverways were covered in dense forests, marshland, and bogs. Only the Jutland peninsula and southern Sweden could have been described as easily farmable. In contrast were the islands of the North Atlantic, where inhabitants depended more on water than soil for sustenance. One

---

109. Roesdahl, *The Vikings*, 27–31, 107–10.

noteworthy exception was the exceptionally volcanic Iceland, where every eruption reshaped the world with searing floods of blazing, liquid earth.[110]

Given the conditions facing the Nordic peoples, it is no surprise they developed the robust hospitality customs and trade networks that they are famed for. These harsh conditions fostered systems of exchange, mutual aid, and reciprocity that were necessary for sustaining societies of any sort in these lands of extremes. They also forced groups into conflict as extended families, villages, and early polities often referred to as tribes fought over very limited pools of resources. These conditions were also likely significant influences on the systems of thralldom, a form of slavery in which people were either enslaved temporarily as restitution for a crime or taken as war captives, and the different gender norms of the Scandinavian peoples in contrast to later societies and their Christian, Frankish neighbors. In a world where survival depended on cooperation, lives could not be wasted needlessly, and banishment from the safety of the community was a death sentence in all but name.[111]

What is consistent in climate and environment are patterns of dramatic change followed by periods of somewhat consistent, though not totally predictable, conditions. Life regularly swung from plenty to scarcity, punctuated by retreat and renewal depending on season and circumstance. The only real certainties that existed were those that were actively created and sustained by people working together to support each other in a harsh ecosystem. Conflict driven by sheer necessity, such as Odin's revolt against Ymir, had the potential to completely reshape lives and communities into totally new arrangements. Such stakes explain why Ragnarök is presented as such a stark, existential crisis beyond all other godly clashes.

These same conditions also drove a sort of synthesis in the aftermath of war and winter. In the case of daily life, the work that went into surviving winter became the old bones used to build a new life in the coming spring. A poor harvest meant less food security, hungry bellies, and a more precarious existence just as a successful trading or raiding expedition carried the promise of more

---

110. Roesdahl, *The Vikings*, 27–31, 107–10.

111. Ingrid Mainland and Colleen Batey, "The Nature of the Feast: Commensality and the Politics of Consumption in Viking Age and Early Medieval Northern Europe," *World Archaeology* 50, no. 5 (2018): 783–90; Price, *Children of Ash and Elm*, 141–43.

comfortable times. On a more societal level, the vanquished in conflict were often subjected to thralldom, some of whom were integrated as full members of the communities of their new rulers.

Early medieval Scandinavian warfare was a far cry from the slash-and-burn, total war destruction, which has become all too familiar in the modern day, as every ship, sword, and seed that could be taken intact was another asset to be used. Even though this dialectical process was never intended on the part of the peoples involved, one can see how, inevitably, the clash of material theses and antitheses gave way to a new synthesis with every turning of the year.

A more naturalistic theory on the origins of Ragnarök that reinforces these dynamics is a particularly cataclysmic one articulated by scholar Neil Price. In *Children of Ash and Elm*, Price argues that Ragnarök could potentially be a cultural memory of a 536 CE cataclysm triggered by a massive volcanic eruption elsewhere on the planet. This event blanketed the skies across Europe with sun-choking ash. According to Price, analyses of tree rings and archeological evidence from the time paints a grim picture of famine, war, and strife as communities dating back to the dawn of the Roman Empire collapsed under the weight of crisis. If such a world-altering event was, indeed, a significant influence on how the Nordic peoples understood their world, then the same patterns already present in their grim environments were likely reinforced and amplified, or even potentially fully realized, as a direct consequence.[112]

Such patterns of new life, growth, retreat, and renewal are also present throughout the natural world. These cycles show strong similarities with other processes such as the water cycle, the cycle of life, and the development of fire ecosystems like the Scandinavian pine forests. There is a certain beauty to the repetition of such patterns throughout Midgard, echoing the deeper music humming through the Nine Worlds. The ebb and flow of wyrd can be felt in many places throughout the natural world, both on the immediate and grand scales. Just as seasons march, rain flows into oceans, and life constantly renews each year, the same can be seen in the great epochs of Earth's history.

Each great geological age of this pale blue dot's history is characterized by great upheaval followed by a new era of life in totally different forms. Multiple epochs spanning millions of years have been uncovered by geologists and

---

112. Price, *Children of Ash and Elm*, 77–81.

paleontologists, with dramatically different life forms and climate systems characterizing each. Every period can trace its evolutionary roots to the previous era, with each period's developments forming the building blocks for the next. Sometimes the transition is one of a preponderance of developments accumulating until the old order was totally displaced by the new, while on five other previous occasions it was accomplished by mass extinctions triggered by cataclysmic changes in the biosphere. The most famous of these was the mass extinction of the dinosaurs, and according to modern biology, we are living in what could become the sixth such catastrophic breakdown of the order of life.[113]

The five mass extinctions in Earth's past are of particular interest for understanding the Nordic creation cycle. Each was caused by a dramatic shift, ranging from large-scale volcanic eruptions blanketing the atmosphere in thick dust to the asteroid that ended the age of the dinosaurs, that utterly upended the conditions for sustaining life. In the aftermath of each of these came a sudden flourishing of new life as the survivors of these disasters spread out, adapted to the new conditions, and filled ecological niches previously dominated by their predecessors. In essence, those who made it into the new worlds that followed the sudden demise of the previous era were now building a redefined existing using the bones of the old.[114]

One can also see a similar pattern in the observed cycles of stellar bodies. Stars are first formed when enormous gravitational forces bring masses of matter and gas together into enormous spheres of energy. This process fires the fusion furnaces that rage in their vast hearts, creating a self-sustaining reaction spanning eons. When they exhaust their considerable fuel reserves, they either implode or go supernova, flinging across space their core elements that seed

---

113. Tammana Begum, "What Is Mass Extinction and Are We Facing a Sixth One?" Natural History Museum, May 19, 2021, https://www.nhm.ac.uk/discover/what-is-mass-extinction-and-are-we-facing-a-sixth-one.html.

114. American Museum of Natural History, "Mass Extinction: What Happened 65 Million Years Ago?" *Dinosaurs: Ancient Fossils, New Discoveries.* May 14, 2005–January 8, 2006. https://www.amnh.org/exhibitions/dinosaurs-ancient-fossils/extinction/mass-extinction; Michael Greshko and National Geographic Staff, "What Are Mass Extinctions, and What Causes Them?" *National Geographic*, September 26, 2019, https://www.nationalgeographic.com/science/article/mass-extinction.

other stars and embed themselves in the core materials of new planets. These enormous conflagrations are theorized to be the source of heavier elements such as iron, platinum, and uranium along with other elements that are necessary for life.[115]

The fierce births and violent deaths of stars embody the same general cycle acted out from Fire and Ice to Ragnarök all the way down to stars seeding and being seeded by the remains of those that came before them. Whether one interprets this process as how the Nordic peoples understood the world around them, as the design of the Powers, or a combination of the two, there is no question these patterns are present throughout physical reality.

The same can be said of humanity. As much as society may feel unchanging and monolithic, the truth of the matter is our social conditions are far more malleable than they appear. Change, upheaval, and building the new using pre-existing conditions as the component materials for what follows are just as constant in history as they are in the physical world. Contrary to the assertions of those who invoke words such as *tradition*, *birthright*, and *custom* to justify any number of claims, much of what we take for granted as long-standing institutions are often products of fairly recent historical developments. Concepts of gender, family, and race have changed over time and across cultures.

Yet even as things change, there are many forms that endure through these changes and developments. This is a direct consequence of the deliberate efforts of people to sustain specific institutions, ideas, and cultural concepts through reinforcement, adaptation, and struggle with those who would replace them with new approaches. Much of what is described as crucial to modern social systems are the products of this constant process of confrontation and adaptation, whether or not their continued survival is justified or defensible. Conflicting developments, including those that challenge these seemingly immovable objects, are themselves shaped both by how they question that which exists and have adapted to better achieve their goals. Eventually, the pressure of such struggles reaches moments when individual components of the social system are forced to give way or, in truly dramatic examples that come closest

---

115. NASA, "What Is a Supernova?" Space Place, last modified July 23, 2021, https://spaceplace.nasa.gov/supernova/en/; Richard Brill, "How Is a Star Born?" *Scientific American*, December 6, 1999, https://www.scientificamerican.com/article/how-is-a-star-born/.

to capturing the creative forces that move wyrd, collapse completely under the pressure of opposing forces that have better adapted to prevailing social and material conditions. As dramatic as these times of total overthrow can be, they are still products of the ørlog laid down by preexisting conditions, including what materials and opportunities are available for constructing the society that follows. Three of the best examples of such moments of total transformation are the Agricultural, Industrial, and Digital Revolutions. Each of these periods was an extended process that completely reshaped human existence and life on Earth in ways that would have been unfathomable at their outset.

The exact causes of the Agricultural Revolution, also known as the Neolithic Revolution, have long been debated by scholars of prehistory. Even so, the general consensus is it began after the end of the last ice age in a warming world with growing swathes of the planet becoming more hospitable for human habitation. These shifts were also much more hospitable to the plants that were the ancestors of the staple crops that have fed much of the world ever since. Early humans began settling down in proximity to these nutritious plants, forming a symbiotic relationship where wild cultivation progressed to small garden plots and later large-scale farms. Similar relationships developed with the predecessors of modern livestock, including chickens, pigs, goats, cattle, and llamas. This process repeated itself in multiple regions of the world with these new societies exporting their inventions through trade, conquest, and other forms of exchange. In each instance, humans created a different way of living by building new possibilities with what was present in their environment.[116]

You could say the same for the next major social and technological leap in human history, known as the Industrial Revolution. The usual story that people are told of the origins of this period typically consists of the brilliance of two eighteenth-century Scottish inventors, Newcomen and Watts, who created the first steam engines to pump water out of coal mines. What tends to be left out in this narrative of individual scientific genius are the broader environmental conditions that forced coal miners into deeper, more flood-prone seams and regions of the British Isles. In the centuries prior to the birth of Newcomen

---

116. Erin Blakemore, "What Was the Neolithic Revolution?" *National Geographic*, April 5, 2019, https://www.nationalgeographic.com/culture/article/neolithic-agricultural -revolution.

and Watts, the growing population of these islands triggered an escalating process of deforestation as people clambered for wood to build homes and fuel fires. These pressures on the woodlands were further accelerated by England's growing colonial and maritime empires, which demanded more wood for building increasingly vast fleets of warships and merchant vessels. Many of these became vital for sustaining the trans-Atlantic slave trade, creating a self-perpetuating cycle that encouraged further consumption, enslavement, and extraction. The result was an environment where wood for heating homes had become incredibly scarce, creating the demand for sending miners into deeper, more dangerous sources of increasingly precious coal.[117]

Though the steam engine is where this story starts, it is hardly where it comes to an end. Industrialization, abetted by the brutality of the enclosure of the commons and the products of colonial exploitation, heralded the birth of a kind of capitalism that completely upended people's lives worldwide.

Old patterns of work, government, leisure, and society were completely rewritten in the first fifty years after the invention of the steam engine, only to be upended with increasing depth in each succeeding generation. The struggle over the fruits of industry has since dominated our world, taking on many different faces and forms even as all are propelled by the same acquisitive scramble that made the steam engine's invention necessary. Even though industrialization totally reshaped humanity, it was itself a product of deeper trends and pressures that predated all the developments we associate with this period. It was through taking these old pressures and existing possibilities that new potential, for good and ill, was unlocked and seemingly unchanging social norms were totally reformed into new patterns.

The same is true of these great epochs as it is of our present, ongoing Digital Revolution. Much like the Agricultural and Industrial Revolutions were products of the bones of the old being shaped into new patterns, the same is true of the explosion of information technology and cyberspace. Initially, computers were used to process huge volumes of data for wealthy corporations, yet there were some engineers, such as those associated with the Stanford Research Institute, who saw greater possibilities in these new inventions. Their optimistic

---

117. Kenneth Pomeranz, *The Great Divergence: China, Europe, and the Making of the Modern World Economy* (Princeton, NJ: Princeton University Press, 2000), 66, 221–23.

vision of using digital technology to enhance human thinking power triggered the race to build the first personal computers and find ways to make these cumbersome contraptions more compact, efficient, and adaptable.[118]

The results are all around us today. Just as social organization and modes of production were inextricably reshaped by agriculture and steam power, the same is true of digital technology. It would not be an exaggeration to say these increasingly compact thinking machines are totally ubiquitous in the present day. Every product of modern society is shaped by them now, including our social relations. These developments saturate all aspects of life and in doing so have bridged divides forged by language, history, political systems, and geography, in effect creating spaces where communities built on affinity could gather more freely. Nothing has hammered home how incredibly transformative the internet and cyberspace are like the enforced physical isolation that came with the COVID-19 pandemic that pushed many to reach out for community through digital space. All these developments are stamped with the ørlog of industrialization while also going beyond what was originally intended to create new, unexpected transformations including creating the ideal social spaces for the modern Pagan movement to thrive. Where this era will lead remains unclear, though, just as the Agricultural and Industrial Revolutions completely displaced seemingly untouchable institutions in their times, and just as digital technology is doing daily. It is quite likely the shape of the world that follows will seem nothing like what came before while still bearing the weight of all that made it possible.

Such broad, epochal changes are not the only examples of little Ragnaröks and Ymir slayings in the human experience. Other, more rapid transformations more commonly associated with the word *revolution* follow similar patterns. Whether one is referring to the French and Russian Revolutions, the Haitian Revolution, anticolonial independence struggles, or even the Arab Spring revolts and the Occupy and Indignados protest movements of 2011 that rocked the world, the same dynamic of existing conditions creating the contradictions that drive transformational change hold true. This does not diminish the role of

---

118. Michael Clarke, "The Digital Revolution," in *Academic and Professional Publishing*, ed. Robert Campbell, Ed Pentz, and Ian Borthwick (Oxford, UK: Chandos Publishing, 2012), 79–80; Emily Wilkerson, "Writing the History of the Digital Revolution," Tulane University, January 30, 2019, https://liberalarts.tulane.edu/newsletter/writing-history-digital-revolution.

human agency in shaping the events that followed—far from it—but rather that human agency is itself constrained by existing ørlog.

Odin's revolt, like the storming of the Bastille, was itself a product of the ørlog laid down by the world under Ymir's rule. That Odin, Vili, and Ve were the ones holding the spears meant they would play a key part in shaping the reality that followed, but their initial rebellion was driven by the circumstances of their existence, much like the starvation and suffering inflicted by indifferent monarchs, the whips of slavers, and imperial masters drove those revolutionary fires the world over. These rebels, much like Odin and the Gods, then found themselves in the position of forging a new world from the remnants of the old with varying results. Such processes of creation, destruction, and recreation were set in motion long before many of the leaders of these rebellions were born, not unlike the three brothers themselves being the third generation since Buri to live under Ymir, yet when the time for reshaping came, they exercised great power over the forms of what followed for good and ill.

This is not to say the Voluspo and Nordic lore somehow prefigured or fore-shadowed these developments. What is present in all these examples are the same patterns that also existed in the world of the pre-Christian Scandinavian peoples on a smaller, more immediate scale. Whether you interpret the lore as a framework developed by the Nordic peoples for understanding the world or as a reflection of the deeper mechanics of all existence that even the gods are bound by, that such patterns are so consistent reinforces how central this dynamic is to understanding modern practice. Wyrd moves, in lore and history, with a distinct, observable rhythm responsible for setting all of existence in mo-tion. That some things, like the deaths of individuals, societies, and even worlds or reality's endlessly transformative potential, are constant does not make our lives a preordained product of a greater, ineffable design. Reality's age-old dance may flow to a consistent tempo, but the beat does not dictate how we take our steps as we move in time to this immanent, eternal song.

Building the New from the Bones of the Old

What these patterns in myth, the natural world, and human history show is all things change, decay, and will eventually die whether they are individual beings, societies, or whole ecological orders. These demises all provide the means for new possibility to be constructed in the wake of ending, creating the seedbed for future potential. This continuously emergent process is shaped both by the actions of everything during its time of living and by the conditions that impact that being, playing out according to the same dynamics in hamingja and ørlog. All these truths confront every person with their own very different, potent moral and philosophical challenges. What is to be done in a world where change is a constant reality and transformative potential is buried in every inhabitant of every world?

It is here that the myths provide some useful starting points. There is a consistent pattern throughout the lore of heroes and gods striking out against those who hoard resources, whether they are material or social, at the expense of everyone around them. These resources are redistributed and the order of existence is brought into alignment with sustaining this new, shared abundance. This tendency is further reinforced by how greed is a consistent driver of conflict throughout the surviving lore, showing a deep disdain for the works of avarice. Such examples also arguably mirror historical developments that were unfolding as the Eddas were being written.

Redistributive logic is present throughout both the sagas and the historical experience of the Nordic peoples. There are many examples in the Eddas of the gods engaging in great acts of generosity and redistribution of wealth, knowledge, and resources while also, in one prominent case, punishing those who deny basic hospitality to others. Easily one of the most noteworthy examples of such redistribution is when the gods collectively create Midgard from Ymir's body in a more abundant, nurturing form than was seen in the age of Ymir. In this instance the gods had total control of the necessary means for crafting a totally new reality, and when they did so, they decided all matters collectively.

They also showed no signs of keeping this great potential solely for themselves. There is even this intriguing passage from the Voluspo that shows this logic of redistribution applies internally as well as externally:

> Then sought the gods their assembly-seats,
> The holy ones, and council held,
> Whether the gods should tribute give,
> Or to all alike should worship belong.[119]

---

119. Bellows, *Poetic Edda*, Voluspo 24.

What makes this verse especially interesting is what options were on the table, regardless of what final decision was ultimately made. The only possibilities up for consideration for how the gods should handle the fruits of worship and offerings are either sharing everything in common or engaging in some form of deliberate, active redistribution of the proceeds among themselves. Nowhere is it even suggested that each god keeps the tribute they receive for themselves alone, as many modern people would expect for any being to do as a matter of course. Even the case of Odin winning the knowledge of the runes follows in this same mold when the hanged god chooses, as described here, to share some of his discovery with beings throughout the Nine Worlds instead of keeping it all for himself:

> Runes shalt thou find, and fateful signs,
> That the king of singers colored,
> And the mighty gods have made;
> Full strong the signs, full mighty the signs
> That the ruler of gods doth write.

> Othin for the gods, Dain for the elves,
> And Dvalin for the dwarfs,
> Alsvith for giants and all mankind,
> And some myself I wrote.[120]

One could argue that reaching this state was what drove Odin, Vili, and Ve to rise against Ymir in the first place. As is described in the Gylfaginning, Ymir was the only being in their state of reality who was allowed to dine on the milk of the great cow Audumla.[121] For Ymir to solely benefit from the fruits of a clear source of wealth is a position that stands clearly at odds with the shared prosperity behind the making of Midgard and the sharing of the runes. Keeping this wealth solely for their own nourishment makes quite the contrast with gods who redistribute tribute among themselves, use the components of the fallen giant to make a more abundant form of reality, and share the fruits of their labor.

---

120. Bellows, *Poetic Edda*, Havamal 143–144.
121. Sturluson, *Prose Edda*, Gylfaginning 6.

In discussing this, it is crucial to address one key point regarding Ymir. Even though it is indisputable that Ymir is the sole beneficiary of Audumla's milk, there is some debate whether Ymir is truly conscious of this process and arguably the great giant is in a state of slumber throughout. If this is the case, then one may see Ymir as a victim of circumstance rather than a deliberate, active propagator of a rather sorry state of affairs. One could even go so far as to claim Ymir's potentially unconscious state makes them guiltless in the arrangement they had come into, and they were only fulfilling their existing role.

What this reasoning misses is how many cases of similar hoarding of wealth in human history are driven less by any deliberate desire to deny resources to others and more by the desire to maintain a highly privileged position. Many a feudal lord, wealthy heir, or corrupt public official has long justified their predation on the grounds of taking their just due with little regard for the consequences or any sort of deliberate plotting to deny wealth to those in need. Whether this is done by extracting the proceeds of labor, quietly accepting the benefits of unearned fortune as theirs by right, or perpetuating a rotten state of affairs by keeping chains of insider dealmaking intact, the result is often little different from those who actively, consciously, and deliberately seek to deprive others of the means of sustenance while being less spectacular in how it manifests.

An unconscious Ymir is one that is still the sole beneficiary of the greatest source of wealth in their state of existence, and their continued exploitation of Audumla's milk perpetuates miserable conditions for all other beings, including their own frost giant children. Ymir's hypothetical slumber is only possible thanks to their monopolistic control over this vital resource and the disruption of this control is necessary for the wealth kept by the great giant to be shared freely.

A more tragic case of greed and consumption is the story of Fenrir. Born a child of Loki and Angrboda, Fenrir's wolfish form was so fearsome that only Tyr was bold enough to care for Asgard's newest resident. As Fenrir grew, his form continuously expanded until the wolf's jaws were so vast that, when opened, they reached from the ground to the edge of the sky. The great wolf's appetites kept up with his swelling shape, leading the gods to fear that soon Fenrir's hunger would become so great that it would consume everything in existence. This fear drove the gods to bind him and use Fenrir's trust of Tyr in an act of betrayal that guaranteed the great wolf's eternal hatred. Though this whole sorry episode is fraught with uncertainty and treachery, these actions were motivated by a desire to preserve the world from the hunger of one, even as the particulars of how this was achieved were rather morally dubious to say the least.[122]

The Volsungasaga provides further depth and nuance on these themes as shown through the havoc unleashed by the Rhinegold treasure. From the moment Fafnir and Regin fought for control of the wealth, with Fafnir's treacherous greed transforming the dwarf into a fearsome dragon, this glimmering prize would bring nothing but strife. Sigurdr's victory over Fafnir and newfound wealth inspired Atli to struggle against the Volsung for control of this great wealth, leading to Sigurdr's death and a bloody feud between his followers and Atli's. The fighting only comes to an end when Gunnar makes the conscious choice to let Atli kill him moments after ensuring he was the only living person who knew the location of the treasure, guaranteeing it would be lost for all time. Gudrun cements this by burning Atli's hall as he and his followers slumbered, putting an end to the ambitious warrior. The final resolution of the Volsungasaga makes it clear this treasure was never worth all the bloodshed it caused, and the conflict only ceases when all knowledge of the Rhinegold is utterly expunged from the world and Atli destroyed.

Further support of such a reading of these sagas and myths lies in the historical context of when they were most likely composed. Early medieval Scandinavia was fraught with conflicts of many kinds, chief among them between a new, rising warrior aristocracy and the more traditional forms of self-governance and ownership, as expressed in the Thing assemblies, which were the norm throughout the Nordic-inhabited parts of the region. As successful raiders and traders accumulated wealth from loot and slaving, this conflict intensified. Ambitious leaders needed the promise of treasure to attract followers and sustain their own personal armies, necessitating the creation of more coercive, centralized power apparatuses that could funnel the necessary resources into a smaller set of hands. This early state-formation process drove significant changes to these societies as victories on the battlefield were cemented with a reordering

---

122. Sturluson, *Prose Edda*, Gylfaginning 34.

of social conditions, as best shown with the example of the creation of the kingdom of Norway.[123]

This particular story begins with Harald Fairhair, the first of many inhabitants of Norway who would succeed in imposing control over the entire region. Much is said in surviving accounts of Harald's martial prowess, which was without a doubt decisive in establishing control, but equally vital for his new regime's success was how he reshaped land ownership. Like many other medieval warlords, Harald seized long-held lands from the peoples who opposed him to redistribute to his loyal followers or keep as his own personal property.[124] With this act, Harald effectively replaced a more communal form of land ownership where estates were held collectively by the families who lived on them with one much closer to the more personal, direct forms of ownership practiced in Frankish-influenced Europe.

Nothing makes this point more strongly than the rebellion by Hakon the Good against Harald's successor, a revolt that was made possible in part by Hakon's promise to restore traditional land rights to their original owners.[125] Olaf II's death at the hands of angry Norwegians centuries later followed a reign characterized by forced conversions and the elimination of redistributive pre-Christian feasts, showcasing similar tensions.[126] Such conflicts, driven by control over land and wealth as much as they were by religion, raged across Scandinavia as social conditions were transformed into a more recognizably feudal form. At the center of this struggle was the very real clash between a more collective, redistributive form of social organization and a hierarchical, privately controlled arrangement that forced the many to make even greater, involuntary sacrifices to sustain the few.

These clashes, both mythic and historic, show rather clearly what the necessary conditions are for justifying reshaping the existing order. Significant imbalances, caused by acts of greed, motivate individuals and groups to strike out for something better. Sometimes these imbalances are deeply rooted, as shown by

---

123. Roesdahl, *The Vikings*, 70–71; Ferguson, *The Vikings*, 46–57; Price, *Children of Ash and Elm*, 77–83.

124. Sturluson, *Heimskringla*, Saga of Harald Harfager 6.

125. Sturluson, *Heimskringla*, Hakon the Good's Saga 2, 11, 17.

126. Sturluson, *Heimskringla*, Olaf Haraldsson's Saga 236–40.

the passage of three generations from the unearthing of Buri by Audumla's foraging to the rising of the three brothers, while in other cases they could be very immediate changes. Following the abolition of the previous, greed-sustained order, a new system is established that actively redistributes resources as widely as possible, which is then actively sustained by the people who created it. This pattern of conflict spurred by the hoarding of wealth, which is settled through sharing this abundance, both shows what causes such upheavals and suggests the best possible resolution.

You can also see the specific case of Ragnarök as a warning. This possibility is quite clearly visible in how the events of this tumultuous conflict are described in the saga, many of which are developments that were clearly seen as incredibly negative by the Nordic peoples. This can be seen most strongly in the description of the war of all against all. Kinslaying, one of the worst of crimes in this society, runs rampant:

> Brothers shall fight and fell each other,
> And sisters' sons shall kinship stain;
> Hard is it on earth, with mighty whoredom;
> Axe-time, sword-time, shields are sundered,
> Wind-time, wolf-time, ere the world falls;
> Nor ever shall men each other spare.[127]

This is only the beginning of a continuous escalation that ends with the total demise of all things in reality:

> The sun turns black, earth sinks in the sea,
> The hot stars down from heaven are whirled;
> Fierce grows the steam and the life-feeding flame,
> Till fire leaps high about heaven itself.[128]

What particularly stands out in this description is the lack of any sense of there being a victor in this struggle. Even though a green new world emerges

---

127. Bellows, *Poetic Edda*, Voluspo 45.

128. Bellows, *Poetic Edda*, Voluspo 57.

from the ashes, Vidar avenges Odin, the children of Thor take up their father's hammer, and Baldr rises from Helheim, the great dragon Nidhoggr remains and the only real implication from this resolution is the cycle will go on.

This stands in stark contrast to a far more well-known example of apocalyptic literature better known as the book of Revelation. This work, which some have argued could be seen as a very thinly veiled attack on the institutions of the Roman Empire, has a far more triumphalist tone that celebrates the defeat of the enemies of God.[129] Revelation, unlike the Voluspo, has a clear message of hope for the faithful and the threat of damnation for their enemies, as shown here, where the text celebrates the downfall of their enemies, personified as the Whore of Babylon:

> After these things I heard something like a loud voice of a great multitude in heaven, saying, "Hallelujah! Salvation, glory, and power belong to our God: for true and righteous are his judgments. For he has judged the great prostitute, her who corrupted the earth with her sexual immorality, and he has avenged the blood of his servants at her hand." A second time they said, "Hallelujah! Her smoke goes up forever and ever." The twenty-four elders and the four living creatures fell down and worshiped God who sits on the throne, saying, "Amen! Hallelujah!" A voice came forth from the throne, saying, "Give praise to our God, all you his servants, you who fear him, the small and the great!"[130]

One can feel the text gloating over the inevitable demise that awaits the vanquished and all the world's dead when Final Judgment is issued from God's throne:

---

129. Gonzalo Rojas-Flores, "The Book of Revelation and the First Years of Nero's Reign," *Biblica* 85, no. 3, (2004), 376–80; Barbara Rossing, "Apocalyptic Violence and Politics: End-Times Fiction for Jews and Christians," *Reflections*, spring 2005, https://reflections.yale.edu/article/end-times-and-end-gamesis-scripture-being-left-behind/apocalyptic-violence-and-politics-end.

130. Revelation 19:1–5 (World English Bible).

I saw a great white throne, and him who sat on it, from whose face the earth and the heaven fled away. There was found no place for them. I saw the dead, the great and the small, standing before the throne. Books were opened. Another book was opened, which is the book of life. The dead were judged out of the things which were written in the books, according to their works. The sea gave up the dead who were in it. Death and Hades gave up the dead who were in them. They were judged, each one according to his works. Death and Hades were thrown into the lake of fire. This is the second death, the lake of fire. If anyone was not found written in the book of life, he was cast into the lake of fire.[131]

The contrast with the Voluspo's celebration of survival, new possibility, and the healing of harms could not be starker:

> In wondrous beauty once again
> Shall the golden tables stand mid the grass,
> Which the gods had owned in the days of old,
>
> Then fields unsowed bear ripened fruit,
> All ills grow better, and Baldr comes back;
> Baldr and Hoth dwell in Hropt's battle-hall,
> And the mighty gods: would you know yet more?[132]

Further contrasts can be seen between how the Voluspo treats the awfulness of the struggles leading up to Ragnarök and the borderline bloodthirsty exultation seen in Revelation at the slaughter that will follow the coming of Christ:

I saw an angel standing in the sun. He cried with a loud voice, saying to all the birds that fly in the sky, "Come! Be

---

131. Revelations 20:11–15 (World English Bible).

132. Bellows, *Poetic Edda*, Voluspo 61–62.

gathered together to the great supper of God, that you may eat the flesh of kings, the flesh of captains, the flesh of mighty men, and the flesh of horses and of those who sit on them, and the flesh of all men, both free and slave, and small and great." I saw the beast, and the kings of the earth, and their armies, gathered together to make war against him who sat on the horse, and against his army. The beast was taken, and with him the false prophet who worked the signs in his sight, with which he deceived those who had received the mark of the beast and those who worshiped his image. They two were thrown alive into the lake of fire that burns with sulfur. The rest were killed with the sword of him who sat on the horse, the sword which came forth out of his mouth. All the birds were filled with their flesh.[133]

The closest possible parallel is the calm assurance that Odin will stand avenged by his son Vidar, but the difference in tone is stark:

> Then comes Sigfather's mighty son,
> Vithar, to fight with the foaming wolf;
> In the giant's son does he thrust his sword
> Full to the heart: his father is avenged.[134]

Even though he achieves victory over his father's killer, this is treated less as a moment of triumph and more one of grim, justified resolution. Totally absent is any of the crowing of total domination over one's foes that rings loud and clear in the angel's pronunciation of doom for the armies of the Beast.

In short, Ragnarök could not be any further from Armageddon if you were actively trying to craft its antithesis. Ragnarök shows an understanding of the world that is cyclical and constantly growing, while more Christian-influenced apocalypses treat this as the final conclusion of the grand epic of creation. Ragnarök is also, in contrast to Armageddon that will come "as a thief in the

---

133. Revelation 19:17–21 (World English Bible).

134. Bellows, *Poetic Edda*, Voluspo 54.

night," a product of actions leading clearly to a discernible conclusion. The central tragedy of Ragnarök as consequences of the actions of the Aesir and circumstances in Midgard makes for a very different understanding of reality than the clear, fixed narrative of inevitable triumph in Revelations. Its fundamental assumption of all involved actors exerting genuine agency stands apart from the very top-down visions of Final Judgment.[135]

If you view this broader cycle as a warning to be heeded, then the signs of Ragnarök could be seen as the symptoms of a dying order in need of replacement. Such manifestations are directly harmful to many and in their own way urge people on to act, particularly when there is a clear source for such ills. If Ragnarök and other similar changes in the fate of whole worlds are the result of deliberate action against the existing order, then the bigger question is what is meant to replace these crumbling realities.

Surviving source material is rather clear and almost paradisical in their descriptions of what comes after the end of Ymir and again following the burning of the Nine Worlds. After Odin, Vili, and Ve overthrew Ymir, they came together to collectively craft a new world as described in the Voluspo 7 and 8. This pattern repeats after the fires of Ragnarök die down, giving way to new promise and new potential in Voluspo 61 and 62.

What is consistent in both cases is the description of these moments of new creation as fertile and defined by ease rather than strife and need. They even have games that survive Ragnarök for passing the time in their utopic conditions. Many who treat the Nordic peoples as violent and grim may find these depictions of ease and prosperity surprising. If conflict and strife were seen as ideal conditions, then it would make sense for godly realms to reflect that. Instead, they envisioned such realms as places of plenty, ease, and safety where all are free to build, play, or rest as they choose.

What makes this point especially important is how the gods deliberately chose to shape their realms in this fashion. As it says in the Voluspo,

> Then sought the gods their assembly-seats,
> The holy ones, and council held;
> Names then gave they to noon and twilight,

---

135. 1 Thessalonians 5:2 (World English Bible).

Morning they named, and the waning moon,
Night and evening, the years to number.[136]

These words implicitly suggest the green world with golden game pieces was the product of deliberate choice and was not some sort of cosmic accident. Understanding these conditions as a deliberate product of godly decisions is thanks to the fundamental malleability of all forms of existence as shown in the forces guiding Nordic cosmology. Even though they were crafting the new from the bones of the old, they still had significant leeway and freedom to shape how these components were utilized. This was just as true whether they were crafting whole realms or giving new life to two dead logs.

This has significant implications for the modern practitioner. Reality in Heathenry does not inherently tend toward doom and gloom. Better worlds are not just possible—they can and have been crafted by the Powers. What has been done before can be done again.

You may, at this point, argue there is a significant difference between the mythic creation of Midgard by the godly Nordic Powers and the actions of humanity. This is, to an extent, certainly true. No one, to date, has managed feats of creation like igniting a sun or spinning planets from bits of stellar matter. On a superficial level it is easy to dismiss the example of gods crafting paradises as an ideal that could never be realized in our waking lives.

This, however, understates how much impact humanity has on our environment. All modern scientific consensus on climate change argues the main drivers of our warming planet are fossil fuel emissions. These emissions continue to climb despite the availability of alternative technologies and methods of social organization that would be less destructive. We further live in a world with technological devices that would've been seen as magical even a hundred years ago, where information flows in global torrents while ship-sized digging machines tear through mountains with ease. We may not have the means to craft whole worlds from the essence of the cosmos, but we, as a species, most certainly have the means to dramatically transform the world we live in.

What does this mean for you living in this warming, increasingly chaotic world? The Radical Heathen answer is to meet this despair head-on with defiant

---

136. Bellows, *Poetic Edda*, Voluspo 6.

vision and action. Our individual and collective choices matter. The state of the world is not fixed, and though we are all doomed to die someday, we still have room to shape what we do with every moment we have between our first and last breaths. Even if the only way to resist is laughing in the face of the inevitable, you will, in that moment, be showing another way is possible and reminding all that we can take our collective destiny into our own hands.

exercise
BREATHING FIRE AND ICE

This next exercise will help you loosen the hard lines imposed by the world around you. Breathing Fire and Ice brings the Powers of creation into you and circulates their primal energies through you. This helps shift your consciousness to better appreciate what they represent and the broader world they helped make. This exercise can also be used to give yourself a burst of energy for mystical workings or to help swiftly shift focus in times of stress and difficulty.

Begin with Understanding the Breath in appendix I. Continue this exercise until you have reached an even, resting pace.

Take a deep breath all the way to the ends of your fingers and toes. Hold this breath for a count of nine before slowly releasing it to the count of nine.

Take a second breath. As you do, visualize the Elder Futhark rune of ice, Isa, and chant its name. Feel everything you associate with this primordial power as its energy spreads throughout your body. Hold this breath for the count of nine before then breathing out on the count of nine, letting the ice leave you.

Take a third breath. As you do, visualize the Elder Futhark Rune of fire, Kenaz, and chant its name. Feel everything you associate with this mighty force as the energy fills your form. Hold this breath for the count of nine before breathing out the flame on a count of nine, letting the fire leave you.

Take a fourth breath. As you do, imagine the forces of Fire and Ice entering your form and taking space in opposite sides of you. You could visualize these forces as splitting you from head to toe, harlequin-style, bisecting you at your waist, or even taking up separate pockets throughout you.

As you hold the previous breath for a count of nine, feel these forces separate from each other as a void feels in the space between heat and frost.

Now breathe out, and as you do, let these two forces rush through the void and collide. Feel their joining fill you as you breathe out.

Take a fifth breath to the count of nine. As you pull in this breath, feel the energies released by the meeting of fire and ice within you fill your entire Self. Hold your breath for the count of nine and feel this potential permeate all aspects of you.

Breathe out to the count of nine and feel the energy flow through you and out into the world. Sit in the moment that follows and focus on how it has made you feel different or what may have surfaced during this exercise. If you are using this to sustain a working, then focus the energy of the moment into your breath, and as it flows out of you, feel it enter the working, providing it with hamingja and raw potential.

CONCLUSION

I began outlining this book just after the early 2020 lockdowns as Black Lives Matter marched in record numbers across the United States. I am now finishing it as the first shots of renewed war on trans lives and abortion rights were fired. Decades passed in weeks as shocking cruelty and stunning possibility were realized in equal measure. There were times when, it seemed, nothing was true and everything was permitted for both good and ill.

These times are certainly troubling ones. It would be dishonest to claim otherwise. Many forms of seemingly fixed, immovable ørlog have revealed their flawed and rotten foundations. Though great injustice reigns, the potential for even greater justice has consistently shined through. If, after all, it is possible for Heathenry to emerge after our source of inspiration was forcibly suppressed by a tide of fire and steel nearly a thousand years ago, then any number of things could be possible, including ending the fear and uncertainty brought on by these days.

Even though we are living in a world that is changing for the worse, that does not diminish our potential to change it for the better. Heathenry embraces this possibility and even if that hope may seem foolish, sometimes that is all you need to open the door for better things. I hope you take what is in this book to make something better of your lives, your communities, and this fragile Earth that we all share. Whether your deeds are great or small, all acts in pursuit of a better world can accumulate to something much bigger in ways that may only become clear in the fullness of wyrd.

appendix I
EXERCISES

The following exercises are the core of Fire and Ice utiseta. Each exercise provides practitioners with the tools for entering a controlled altered state of consciousness, also known as the ecstatic state. All the exercises in this book are built on the following meditations.

exercise
UNDERSTANDING THE BREATH

Understanding the Breath is the foundational exercises for all forms of Fire and Ice meditative, trance, and ecstatic practice. Its purpose is to help your body reach a resting, relaxed state that makes it easier to reach an altered state of consciousness. Understanding the Breath slows your body down, making it easier to focus your attention inward and outward.

Begin by finding a quiet space where you can sit comfortably.
Breathe normally at a relaxed pace.
Close your eyes.
Take a slow, deep breath in through your nose. As you draw in your breath, slowly count to nine. Your breath should begin at number one and finish at number nine. Hold your breath for a slow count from number one to number nine.
When you have reached number nine while holding your breath, begin to slowly exhale through your mouth, counting down from

number nine to number one. Begin breathing out on number nine and completely empty your lungs of air.

This process of breathing in to the count of nine, holding for the count of nine, and breathing out to the count of nine is one breath cycle.

Begin a second breath cycle. On this cycle, focus on how your lungs feel as they fill with air, hold breath, and release it.

Now begin a third breath cycle. On this cycle, focus on how your heartbeat feels during each stage of the cycle. Pay attention to what causes it to speed up and slow down.

If you need to repeat the second or third cycles to better observe how these parts of your body feel, go right ahead. You should not rush ahead to the next step until you have a firm sense of what is taking place during each cycle. What matters is feeling and understanding the interactions between your breath, your heart, and your lungs.

Once you are comfortable with what you are sensing during the second and third cycles, begin a fourth breath cycle. In this one, focus on how the rest of your body feels during each stage of the cycle. Do you feel tense during some moments and relaxed during others? How does it feel when your heart speeds up and slows down? Pay attention to what you sense during these moments.

exercise

CALMING THE SEA AND SKY

Calming the Sea and Sky is frequently used in Fire and Ice practice as a grounding exercise in preparation for ecstatic work. It gives any stresses in your thoughts and emotions space to play out, clearing the way for further trance work. Calming the Sea and Sky can also be used outside of trance as a tool for reaching a state of emotional and mental equilibrium. This exercise can be challenging for newer practitioners. Do not be discouraged by how swiftly or slowly the sea and sky clear for you, what is important is giving these tensions the space to work themselves out.

Begin with the Understanding the Breath exercise. Perform as many breath cycles as necessary to reach a relaxed state before beginning the next step.

Once you are relaxed, close your eyes and visualize the open ocean with the sky above it. Let everything in your visualization begin to move on its own. Do not focus on creating waves, ripples from the wind, or motion in the sky. Simply let it happen in a way that feels most natural.

When you feel everything is moving on its own, you may begin with the next element of this meditation. This part is a bit tricky to realize, so take as much time as you need to get it right.

In the space you have visualized in your mind, allow your feelings and stresses to seep into very specific spaces.

Let your thinking, worries, and concerns be reflected in the sky as stormy weather. The more occupied your mind is, the more ferocious the storm in the sky should be.

As the sky becomes a mirror of your mind, let your feelings, emotions, and stresses manifest in the oceans. The size, speed, and consistency of the waves and motion of the sea should match your distress, concerns, and feelings.

Allow these elements of your visualization to manifest uncontrolled. Let the mirrors of sea and sky take shape on their own and do not force their conditions to match your expectations. What determines if what you are visualizing matches your internal state is when it feels most appropriate.

It is now time to part the storm and calm the seas. Feel what is driving the forces causing the storm. There may be one root cause or many. As you begin to process the causes of the storm, allow this to change the vision. As your thoughts become clear, let the clouds part, and as you better understand your emotions let the seas calm. Continue this process until you are rewarded with a sunny sky (or if you prefer, a starry night sky) and calm waters.

This meditation is useful for other work, but it should never be seen or used as a replacement for long-term therapy and other such practices. If you find it helpful in such matters, use it, but this should never be a replacement for seeking professional help. This exercise will be challenging at first but will become easier with practice.

exercise

THE WORLD TREE WITHIN

The World Tree Within is used for utiseta journeying and as preparation for seiðr spellwork and deathwork. The practitioner invokes the closest material representations of extreme heat and cold, the earth's core and outer space, to circulate the energies of creation between them and what lies beyond yourself. This makes it easier to conduct journeying and can be useful for reaching the dead or vættir during workings.

Begin with the Understanding the Breath exercise. Once you have completed all the cycles outlined in that exercise, move on to the Calming the Sea and Sky exercise. When you have reached a state of restful calm, you may proceed to the next step.

Focus your mind and your feelings on your spine. Feel it running from the base of your skull down to your tailbone. Feel the nerves that run through the spine and branch outward from it into the rest of your body.

Now place your focus on the base of the spine and your tailbone. Push your attention beneath you, pressing down into the ground under you. Visualize your focus moving through the earth below like roots pushing into the soil.

Continue going deeper and deeper, feeling the rocks and heat as you go. Press your visualization on until you reach the earth's molten core. Feel the fiery heart pulsing in the depths of the earth.

Bring your attention steadily back to yourself while keeping awareness of the heat in the earth's core within you.

Shift your focus to the crown of your skull. Push your visualization upward into the sky, feeling your awareness grow like the trunk and branches of a great tree. As you go, feel the coolness of the wind and air around you.

Keep pushing your awareness until it goes beyond the limits of the atmosphere into the cold of the space beyond the sky's edge.

Feel the deep, primordial chill of the stellar vacuum that lies beyond the earth's embrace.

While feeling the heat in the roots of your awareness and the cold at the outermost branches, pull both feelings into yourself as swiftly as possible. Feel these opposing forces move through the limits of your extended awareness as they race toward your body. As they move, pull the roots and branches of your awareness back into yourself.

Slam both energies together within yourself. Feel the raw energy, the opening of potential and the reenactment of the moment of creation within you. Let this feeling fill your physical body, your mind, and your awareness. As you do this, perform one breath cycle.

When you have finished these breaths, sit with the new feeling inside you for a moment, open your eyes, and begin the work.

exercise
GOING TO THE WELLS

Going to the Wells is a basic utiseta exercise intended for people who are just getting started in their practice or are seeking to commune directly with the wisdom that can be found in the wells. It guides you down the World Tree to the Three Wells at the base of Yggdrasil, a place that is described in the *Prose Edda* as a crossroads between the Nine Worlds. This makes it a useful starting place for any utiseta journeywork and a safe place for beginning your explorations of the Otherworlds.

Begin by finding a calm, undisturbed place for doing the working. Make sure there are no potential distractions when you first practice this exercise. With experience this can be done in places like public parks or even in a busy crowd.

Conduct the Understanding the Breath exercise. Complete as many breath cycles as you feel are necessary until your heart reaches a resting state.

Once you have reached a resting state, begin the Calming the Sea and Sky exercise. When you are doing Going to the Wells, make sure you continue the Sea and Sky exercise until the sea is smooth as glass and the sky is completely clear. When engaging in utiseta, it is critical you are as calm and relaxed as possible. This makes you more receptive to what may come during the work.

Perform the World Tree Within exercise from earlier in this appendix. After you have completed this exercise and held the extremes of void and core within, you may proceed to the next step.

Feel the version of the World Tree that has just been running through you. Imagine you are now on the tree, holding on to the trunk and its branches.

Ask your fylgja to manifest beside you.

Visualize yourself climbing down the tree until you reach where the trunk meets the soil Yggdrasil is planted in.

Walk along the base until you see a great, open pool before you. This is the Well of Urdr. In the lore, it is said those who wish to drink from it must sacrifice something in exchange. For the purposes of this exercise, you will not be doing this.

Gaze deep into the well. Let whatever images surface run through your mind. Pay attention to what you see but do not try to analyze. Allow what emerges from the well to flow freely through you.

When you feel you have seen enough imagine yourself stepping away from the well. Feel your body again, take a deep breath and awaken. Think on what you experienced and its potential meaning.

With practice, it is possible to approach the well seeking guidance for specific questions or problems by fixing them in your mind as you climb the tree. Such an approach should be conducted later with time and experience. While you are starting out, focus on reaching the well and taking in what you see.

When you feel you have seen enough, imagine yourself stepping away from the well. Feel your body again, take a deep breath, and awaken. Think on what you experienced and its potential meaning.

appendix II
SOURCE MATERIALS

Many of the concepts described in this book draw their inspiration from a range of written sources that preserved the core stories of Nordic myth. This appendix is a short summary of the myths referenced in this book and where they come from. Two of the best sources of saga material are the Icelandic Saga Database (https://sagadb.org/) and the Stofnun Árna Magnússonar (https://www.arnastofnun.is/en/front-page), both of which provide English translations of most sagas and have digital scans of core texts such as the *Poetic Edda*.

Many of these sources were first produced more than five hundred years ago and were compiled at the behest of the powerful and influential of their times and places. The revival of interest during the 1800s meant much of the initial scholarship was heavily influenced by the Victorian Era's nationalist and imperializing biases. Later scholarship has sought to correct this with a wealth of archeological, historical, and linguistic research. Earlier images of a bloodthirsty, inherently violent, and ruthless people have been pushed aside by a far more nuanced and humanizing understanding of the ancients and their works. Even so, the original texts still reflect the class and newly medieval Christian biases of their times and should be read with a critical eye.

Myth works on many different levels. What happens in these stories is both true and representative of larger concepts and cosmic functions. This is especially true of the Nordic myths that have a poetic style that was highly reference-dependent, indirect, and metaphorical. A good way to think of this is like how you need to know a bit about modern pop and subcultural references along with modern digital culture to understand many online memes. I recommend you consider what these stories show in their linear narratives, broader patterns, and symbolic potential. This will give you a richer, fuller understanding of how these myths hold truth across the ages.

The Eddas, Sagas, and Folklore

The Eddas, sagas, and folklore of the Nordic peoples are the core source materials for modern practitioners. Each of these bodies of material was preserved and recorded well after conversion, with the Eddas being the oldest surviving sources describing the Nordic myths. I strongly recommend you read an introductory text on Nordic myth before engaging with these sources, as they can be somewhat inaccessible for anyone who is new to these materials.

The Eddas consist of two different written works that are known as the *Poetic Edda* and the *Prose Edda*. The *Poetic Edda* was a collection of Nordic sagas that were recorded in Iceland at some point in the 1200s CE and were brought together as a single codex known as the *Codex Regius,* or the *Konungsbók Eddukvæða*, a gift for the King of Denmark and Norway in 1663 CE. Their authorship is unknown, and they are some of the only written sources produced by pre-Christian Nordics.

The *Prose Edda*, by contrast, was written by Iceland statesman and antiquarian Snorri Sturluson as a thirteenth-century manual for teaching Icelandic poetry. It includes information on many of the Nordic gods and core stories but also contains some of Sturluson's biases, such as his depiction of the gods as humans from Troy.

The sagas are other poems and stories that were first recorded beginning in the 1200s CE. These often recorded specific warriors, famous ancestors, and other stories the Christian Scandinavian feudal aristocracy saw as worth preserving. The sagas contain a lot of information on the norms, word usage, and core assumptions of the Nordic peoples that are also present in the Eddas and provide further examples of kennings present in both. Some of the most famous sagas are the Icelandic Book of Settlements, the Saga of Erik the Red, the Saga of Grettir the Strong, and the Saga of Ragnar Loðbrok.

Folklore has the most variety and can be found in collections compiled by interested folklorists. These sources vary considerably, especially because they were often recorded well after conversion. They are, however, some of the best surviving information on the animistic Nordic Powers. Folklore provides an invaluable bottom-up view of Nordic spiritual practices that contrasts with the more elite-oriented Eddas and sagas.

The Nordic Gods

Nordic myth, like many other forms of pre-Christian myth, has many polytheistic gods who are described in the Eddas. Most of the Nordic deities gather together in one of three groups, which are known as the Aesir, Vanir, and Jötnar, while a few, referred to here as the Others, stand apart from the rest. These groups are each associated with different facets of reality and can be viewed as a metaphor for the relationship between humanity and the natural world. More information on these gods can be found in *The Way of Fire and Ice* by Ryan Smith, *A Practical Heathen's Guide to Asatru* by Patricia Lafayllve, *Gods and Myths of Northern Europe* by H. R. Ellis Davidson, and other sources on Nordic mythology.

The Aesir are the Nordic gods who are most associated with human society with connections to concepts like war, justice, agriculture, and language. Some of the most well-known Aesir are Odin, Thor, Tyr, and Loki. This clan of deities is sometimes in conflict with the Jötnar, though many of the Aesir have Jötun parentage, and these two groups freely intermarry.

The Vanir are often called the Nordic gods of nature, though this is something of a simplification. They are associated with ways humans interact with their environment, such as sailing, fertility, and magic. Some of the most well-known Vanir are Freyr, Freya, and Njord. The Vanir are described as more mystically potent and have close ties to the alfar.

The Jötnar, referred to individually as Jötun, are often referred to as the giants and can be seen as the Nordic gods of the wilderness. Some of the most well-known Jötnar are Surtr, Ymir, Jord, and Skaði. They are associated with fire, ice, storms, and the earth itself. Though they are often hostile and at odds with the Aesir and Vanir, they also share hospitality with them and intermarry.

The Others are the deities who are associated with primal forces like time and death. They stand apart from the other groups of gods. Some of the most well-known of the Others are the Norns, Hel, Nidhoggr, and Fenrir.

The Volsungasaga

The Volsungasaga is one of the most celebrated epics in Germanic literature that has been adapted, translated, and reimagined many times since it was first recorded. Its central figures are Sigurðr the dragonslayer, Brunhildr, the dragon Fafnir, Regin, and Atilla the Hun, who is referred to in the text as Atli. The sagas that make up the Volsungasaga make up at least a third of the *Poetic Edda*'s contents, including but not limited to Sigrdrifumol, Fafnismol, Sigurtharkvitha en Skamma, Atlakvitha en Gronlënzka, and Guthrunarhvot, all of which have events that are referenced in this book. The Volsungasaga seems to have been one of the most widely shared and adapted epics in Nordic myth, as shown by the different versions of specific elements of the story preserved in the *Poetic Edda*.

At the center of the story is the Rhinegold treasure, which was taken from the gods by Andvari, cursed by Loki, and then given as payment to a man named Hreithmar. This curse drives those who possess it into strife and conflict, beginning with Hreithmar's death at the hands of his son Fafnir, who slowly transforms into a dragon obsessed with guarding the treasure. Fafnir's brother Regin recruits the warrior Sigurðr, whom he will then betray so he can reclaim what he sees as rightfully his, to slay the dragon. Sigurðr is warned of the impending treachery after slaying Fafnir by ambushing the dragon on the advice of a figure often assumed to be Odin in disguise and kills Regin first. He then meets and wakes Brunhildr from an enchanted sleep before becoming a mighty king in his own right and marrying his wife Guðrun.

Sigurðr's wealth and prestige soon attract the eye of the warlord Atli, who wants the Rhinegold at all costs. Sigurðr and Brunhildr are slain in the conflict, while Guðrun is taken captive by Atli. Atli then baits Guðrun's brother Gunnar into an ambush, but Gunnar turns the tables by taking the secret of the treasure's location to the grave. Guðrun, bereft of her love and family, then takes her revenge on Atli by waiting until the warlord's followers are deep asleep and burning them alive in their hall. Greed is a central driver of conflict in this story, which is a theme that is quite common in other parts of Nordic myth.

Saga of Erik the Red and Njal's Saga

The saga of Erik the Red is one of the main Icelandic sources on Nordic expeditions into North America and Greenland, along with the Saga of the Greenlanders. It covers the voyages of Thorfinn Karlsefni, Erik the Red's banishment to Greenland, his son Leif Erikson's Christian evangelism, Erikson's arrival in Vinland (which is suspected by scholars to have been modern-day Newfoundland), and the eventual collapse of the Vinland colony. There are two versions of this saga that survive to the present day and are preserved in the Hauksbok and the Skalholtsbok, both of which seem to derive from a common original first composed in the thirteenth century CE.

The Saga of Erik the Red is especially valuable for modern practitioners because of the highly detailed descriptions it gives of pre-conversion Nordic spiritual practices and sorcery. Its description of the seeress consulted in chapter 4 of the saga is one of the most complete of a Nordic völva in action that survives to the present day. Scholars believe the details were meant, in part, as a polemical attack on these practices, but even though this bias is present, it still nonetheless provides a window into Nordic mystical practices.

Njal's Saga is considered the pinnacle of early medieval Iceland poetry by modern scholars. It tells the story of an extended late tenth century CE blood feud that embroils the island for several decades. Njal's Saga gives one of the best examples of Icelandic legal proceedings, the conditions under which vengeance could be claimed, attitudes toward fate and destiny, and more of the social world of the Nordic Icelanders during this period. It is also one of the best examples of surviving skaldic poetry, making it an invaluable source for any aspiring skald. It, along with Erik the Red's saga, provides an invaluable perspective into the world of pre-Christian Nordic Icelandic philosophy and day-to-day life.

GLOSSARY

alfar: Animistic beings who are more commonly and popularly known as elves. The alfar live both in the realm of Alfheim and, in folkloric sources, different parts of Midgard.

animism: A set of perspectives that argues for treating other living beings, habitats, and spaces as if they possess agency and autonomy that must be respected. In some forms of animism, including Nordic-influenced ones, there are Powers who are associated with specific places, which includes but is not limited to the alfar, the dvergr, and vættir.

bindrunes: A form of runic magic. A bindrune is created by taking more than one rune, which can be from different runic alphabets, and combining them to make a single, new symbol. This symbol can be imbued with a specific purpose that is supported by the runes that make up the bindrune.

blót: The main devotional rite in Radical Norse Paganism. Central to any blót (pronounced like the word *bloat*) is a ritual sacrifice, which is usually food or drink, though it can be any item or creation that is valuable to the person giving the offering.

continuous cosmology: The capstone of a broader understanding of reality and spirituality. It is part of a worldview that emphasizes connection and relationship over separation and dualistic thinking that flows naturally from the surviving source material.

deathwork: Mystical practices focused on communing with the dead.

ecstatic state: An altered state of consciousness that can be reached using a variety of methods, including but not limited to music, dancing, and meditation.

fylgja: Your spiritual shadow. It is your subconsciousness, a reflection of your hidden desires, and an extension of your Self. The fylgja (pronounced *FILL-ge-yah*; the plural, fylgjur, is pronounced *FILL-ge-yur*) is used as a guide and protector in Fire and Ice mysticism, particularly for utiseta journeywork.

gæfu: One of the two parts of hamingja. Gæfu refers to your personal abilities and skills which develop over time.

Ginnungagap: The empty void that existed between the worlds of fire and ice in the time before Ymir.

gipta: One of the two parts of hamingja. Gipta refers to what you are given by your origins.

hamingja: Also known as luck. In Radical Norse Paganism, hamingja (pronounced *ha-ming-ya*) is inherently part of you, made of all your skills, means, immediate conditions, and anything else in your life capable of changing yourself and your circumstances. Hamingja comes from what is passed on to you from the circumstances of your birth by those who came before.

hamr: Your physical form. The root of hamr (pronounced *HAM-er*) is your body, but that is not all there is to hamr. Hamr is your whole form, including how you present yourself, how you dress, the way you move, and your body language.

Heathenry: Heathenry is the most commonly used term of identification by Norse Pagans, with many (though not all) using *Heathen* and *Norse Pagan* interchangeably. However, in Scandinavia and Germany, the term *Heathen* is used the same way as *Pagan* is in the rest of the world.

hugr: Your mind. The hugr (pronounced *HOO-ger*) is thought, feeling, consciousness, and awareness.

Isaz: The name of the Elder Futhark rune of ice.

Jörmungandr: The serpent child of Loki and Angrboða, Jörmungandr (pronounced *YOR-mun-gan-dir*) is said to be so massive that it circles all of reality and holds its tail in its jaws.

Kenaz: The name of the Elder Futhark rune of the torch and fire.

kenning: A way of describing something in poetic terms that includes references to Norse lore, some of which are particularly indirect and obscure. Understanding these kennings is essential for understanding the meaning of the Norse sagas.

kinslaying: The act of killing a close blood relation and one of the worst crimes in the various Nordic societies.

Muspelheim: The land of fire. This was the home of the great flames that rushed into the Ginnungagap countless ages ago and is said to be where the great Jötun Surtr makes their hall.

Nidhoggr: A great dragon whose hunger for the World Tree will never be satisfied and who can never stop chewing at the backbone of reality.

Niflheim: The realm of ice where the surge of frost mixed with flame created the building blocks of reality.

ørlog: This represents the sum of all actions and every individual's capacity to change fate. Ørlog (pronounced *OAR-log*) is made up of all the things in life that have already been determined by past deeds beyond our control, existing elements of society that come about through the accumulation of many actions over time, or the consequences of all actions. This includes the time and place of your birth, your parents, the consequences of others' actions, and the other elements of your life.

reenchantment: The process of finding ways to infuse modern life with a fresh sense of wonder, awe, and beauty.

seiðr: A uniquely Norse form of mysticism that includes forms of channeling, spellwork, and meditation. The word *seiðr* is often translated to mean "witchcraft" or "sorcery" and has linguistic connections to the Old Norse words for spinning and storms.

spae: A form of seiðr where the practitioner, known as a spaeworker, becomes a channel, giving their voice to one of the Powers so they may speak through the spaeworker.

synchronicity: A phenomenon, noted by psychologists, in which largely internal experiences such as dreams or visions during meditation and trance correspond with seemingly coincidental events in the material world.

Things: Things (pronounced *tings*) were the popular assemblies of the ancient Norse peoples that served as law-making bodies and courts for dispute resolution.

thralldom: A Nordic form of slavery. People were enslaved either for a set period as restitution for injuries done against another person or as captives in war.

utiseta: One of the three forms of seiðr. The word means "sitting out" and comes from the Old Norse expression *seti uti til frodleiks,* "sitting out for wisdom." Utiseta is both a form of meditation and a mystical art used for answering challenging questions.

vættr: A vættr (pronounced *vite* and *vie-tear*) is a sacred essence known as a spirit, collectively known as the vættir.

weregild: Compensation for injury and death.

wyrd: The greatest of the Nordic cosmos. It is the symphony of life cocreated by the actions of all beings, from the humblest living things to the mightiest of the godly and animistic Powers of Nordic practice.

Yggdrasil: The center of the Norse Pagan universe, Yggdrasil (pronounced *IGG-druh-sil*), is also known as the World Tree. It supports and sustains all the Nine Worlds of Nordic myth, including our own.

BIBLIOGRAPHY

"About the Soul." Religious Tolerance. Accessed June 11, 2022. https://www
.religioustolerance.org/souldef.htm.

Adams, Tim. "Anxious, Atomised … and Not in It Together: The State of Britain in 2015." *Guardian*, April 19, 2015. https://www.theguardian.com
/society/2015/apr/19/anxious-atomised-not-in-it-together-the-state-of
-britain-2015.

American Museum of Natural History. "Mass Extinction: What Happened
65 million Years Ago?" *Dinosaurs: Ancient Fossils, New Discoveries*. May 14,
2005–January 8, 2006. https://www.amnh.org/exhibitions/dinosaurs
-ancient-fossils/extinction/mass-extinction.

Arcini, Caroline Ahlstom. "The Vikings Bare Their Filed Teeth." *American Journal of Physical Anthropology* 128, no. 4 (2005): 727–33. doi:10.1002/ajpa.20164.

Auryn, Mat. "Synchronicity & the Psychic Witch." Patheos Pagan. June 26, 2017.
https://www.patheos.com/blogs/matauryn/2017/06/26/synchronicity
-witch/.

Beckett, John. "4 Steps to Re-enchant the World." Patheos Pagan. September
3, 2015. https://www.patheos.com/blogs/johnbeckett/2015/09/4-steps
-to-re-enchant-the-world.html.

Begum, Tammana. "What Is Mass Extinction and Are We Facing a Sixth One?"
Natural History Museum. May 19, 2021. https://www.nhm.ac.uk/discover
/what-is-mass-extinction-and-are-we-facing-a-sixth-one.html.

Bek-Pedersen, Karen. *The Norns in Old Norse Mythology*. Edinburgh, UK: Dunedin Academic Press, 2011.

Bellows, Henry Adams, trans. *The Poetic Edda: The Mythological Poems*. Mineola, NY: Dover Publications, 2004.

Blakemore, Erin. "What Was the Neolithic Revolution?" *National Geographic*, April 5, 2019. https://www.nationalgeographic.com/culture/article/neolithic-agricultural-revolution.

Brill, Richard. "How Is a Star Born?" *Scientific American*, December 6, 1999. https://www.scientificamerican.com/article/how-is-a-star-born/.

Byrd, W. Carson, and Matthew W. Hughey. "Born That Way? 'Scientific' Racism Is Creeping Back into Our Thinking. Here's What to Watch Out For." *Washington Post*, September 28, 2015. https://www.washingtonpost.com/news/monkey-cage/wp/2015/09/28/born-that-way-scientific-racism-is-creeping-back-into-our-thinking-heres-what-to-watch-out-for/.

Clarke, Michael. "The Digital Revolution." In *Academic and Professional Publishing*, 79–98. Edited by Robert Campbell, Ed Pentz, and Ian Borthwick. Oxford, UK: Chandos Publishing, 2012.

Davidson, H. R. Ellis. *Gods and Myths of Northern Europe*. New York: Penguin, 1984.

———. *The Road to Hel: A Study of the Conception of the Dead in Old Norse Literature*. New York: Greenwood Press, 1968.

Dasent, George Webbe, trans. *The Story of Burnt Njal—From the Icelandic of the Njals Saga*. London: Grant Richards, 1900.

Dickens, Bruce, ed. *Runic and Heroic Poems of the Old Teutonic Peoples*. Cambridge, UK: Cambridge University Press, 1915.

Doyle, Arthur Conan. *The Sign of the Four*. In *Lippincott's Monthly Magazine*. London: Spencer Blackett, 1890.

Dubois, Thomas A. *Nordic Religions in the Viking Age*. Philadelphia: University of Pennsylvania Press, 1999.

Eriksen, Marianne Hem. "Doors to the Dead: The Power of Doorways and Thresholds in Viking Age Scandinavia." *Archeological Dialogues* 20, no. 2 (2013): 187–214. doi:10.1017/S1380203813000238.

Federici, Silvia. *Caliban and the Witch: Women, the Body, and Primitive Accumulation.* Brooklyn, NY: Autonomedia, 2004.

Ferguson, Robert. *The Vikings: A History.* New York: Penguin Books, 2009.

Fridriksdóttir, Jóhanna Katrín. *Valkyrie: The Women of the Viking World.* London: Bloomsbury Academic, 2020.

Gould, Stephen J. *Ever Since Darwin: Reflections in Natural History.* New York: W. W. Norton and Company, 1977.

Graham, Ruth. "Can Megachurches Deal with Mega Money in a Christian Way?" *Atlantic,* March 12, 2014. https://www.theatlantic.com/business /archive/2014/03/can-megachurches-deal-with-mega-money-in-a -christian-way/284379/.

Greshko, Michael, and National Geographic staff. "What Are Mass Extinctions, and What Causes Them?" *National Geographic*, September 26, 2019. https://www.nationalgeographic.com/science/article/mass-extinction.

Heath, Cat. *Elves, Witches & Gods: Spinning Old Heathen Magic in the Modern Day.* Woodbury, MN: Llewellyn Publications, 2021.

———. "Restoration, Not Reenchantment." *Seo Helrune* (blog), October 29, 2018. https://seohelrune.com/2018/10/29/restoration-not-reenchantment/.

"The Ice Age." NatureScot. Last modified February 18, 2022. https://www .nature.scot/landforms-and-geology/scotlands-rocks-landforms-and-soils /landforms/ice-age-landforms/ice-age.

Jesch, Judith. *Women in the Viking Age.* Rochester, NY: Boydell Press, 2001.

Jones, Gwyn. *A History of the Vikings.* Oxford, UK: Oxford University Press, 1984.

Keller, Jared. "Americans Are Staying as Far Away from Each Other as Possible." Pacific Standard. Last modified June 14, 2017. https://psmag.com

/social-justice/americans-are-staying-as-far-away-from-each-other-as
-possible.

Kennedy, Maev. "British Museum to Go More Than Skin Deep with Scythian
Exhibition." *Guardian,* May 30, 2017. https://www.theguardian.com
/culture/2017/may/30/british-museum-skin-scythian-exhibitio-tattoo
-empire.

"Konungsbók eddukvæða GKS 2365 4to." Stofnun Árna Magnússonar. Accessed December 16, 2022. https://www.arnastofnun.is/is/konungsbok
-eddukvaeda-gks-2365-4to.

Kroll, Luisa. "Megachurches, Megabusinesses." *Forbes,* September 17, 2003.
https://www.forbes.com/2003/09/17/cz_lk_0917megachurch.html?sh
=2e6f55d27489.

Kvideland, Reimund, and Kenning K. Sehmsdorf. *Scandinavian Folk Belief and
Legend.* Minneapolis: University of Minnesota Press, 1988.

Kvilhaug, Maria. "Fylgjur—Guardian Spirits and Ancestral Mothers." *Blade
Honer* (blog). January 29, 2020. https://bladehoner.wordpress.com/2020
/01/29/fylgjur-guardian-spirits-and-ancestral-mothers/.

Lafayllve, Patricia M. *A Practical Heathen's Guide to Asatru.* Woodbury, MN:
Llewellyn Publications, 2013.

Laqueur, Thomas. *Making Sex: Body and Gender from the Greeks to Freud.* Cambridge, MA: Harvard University Press, 1990.

Lewis, Diane. "Anthropology and Colonialism." *Current Anthropology* 14, no. 5
(December 1973): 581–602. https://www.jstor.org/stable/2741037.

Lindow, John. *Trolls: An Unnatural History.* London: Reaktion Books, 2014.

Lyons, Sara. "The Disenchantment/Re-Enchantment of the World: Aesthetics,
Secularization, and the Gods of Greece from Friedrich Schiller to Walter
Pater." *The Modern Language Review* 109, no. 4 (October 2014): 873–95.
doi:10.5699/modelangrevi.109.4.0873.

Mainland, Ingrid, and Colleen Batey. "The Nature of the Feast: Commensality and the Politics of Consumption in Viking Age and Early Medieval

Northern Europe." *World Archaeology*, 50, no. 5 (2018): 781–803. doi:10.1080 /00438243.2019.1578260.

NASA. "What Is a Supernova?" Space Place. Last modified July 23, 2021. https://spaceplace.nasa.gov/supernova/en/.

Nordvig, Mathias. *Ásatrú for Beginners: A Modern Heathen's Guide to the Ancient Northern Way*. Emeryville, CA: Rockridge Press, 2020.

Orchard, Andy. *Dictionary of Norse Myth and Legend*. London: Cassell, 1997.

Orel, Vladimir E. *A Handbook of Germanic Etymology*. Leiden, Netherlands: Brill, 2003.

Perabo, Lyonel D. "Shapeshifting in Old Nordic-Icelandic Literature." *Roda da Fortuna: Revista Eletronica sobre Antiguidade e Medievo* 6, no. 1 (2017): 135–58. https://docs.wixstatic.com/ugd/3fdd18_662e837d9aa04535947ed5dfab f1a435.pdf.

Pomeranz, Kenneth. *The Great Divergence: China, Europe, and the Making of the Modern World Economy*. Princeton, NJ: Princeton University Press, 2000.

Price, Neil. *Children of Ash and Elm: A History of the Vikings*. New York: Basic Books, 2020.

———. *The Viking Way: Magic and Mind in Late Iron Age Scandinavia*. Oxford, UK: Oxbow Books, 2019.

Price, Neil, Charlotte Hedenstierna-Johnson, Torun Zachrisson, Anna Kjellstrom, Jan Stora, Maja Krzewinska, Torsten Gunther, Veronica Sobrado, Mattias Jakobsson, and Anders Gotherstrom. "Viking Warrior Women? Reassessing Birka Chamber Grave Bj.581." *Antiquity* 93, no. 367 (2019): 181–98. doi:10.15184/aqy.2018.258.

Rees, Owen. "Going Berserk: The Psychology of the Berserkers." *Medieval Warfare* 2, no. 1 (2012): 23–26. https://www.jstor.org/stable/48578628.

Robinson, Howard. "Dualism." Stanford Encyclopedia of Philosophy. Last modified September 11, 2020. https://plato.stanford.edu/entries/dualism/.

Roesdahl, Else. *The Vikings*. London: Penguin Books, 2016.

Rojas-Flores, Gonzalo. "The Book of Revelation and the First Years of Nero's Reign." *Biblica* 85, no. 3 (2004): 375–92.

Rossing, Barbara. "Apocalyptic Violence and Politics: End-Times Fiction for Jews and Christians." *Reflections*. Spring 2005. https://reflections.yale .edu/article/end-times-and-end-gamesis-scripture-being-left-behind /apocalyptic-violence-and-politics-end.

Sephton, J., trans. *Saga of Erik the Red*. Icelandic Saga Database. https://sagadb .org/eiriks_saga_rauda.en.

Sheng, Lay. "A Postcolonial Approach to Social Science?" London School of Economics and Political Science. November 22, 2016. https://blogs.lse .ac.uk/government/2016/11/22/a-postcolonial-approach-to-social -science/.

Shippey, Thomas. *Laughing Shall I Die: Lives and Deaths of the Great Vikings*. London: Reaktion Books, 2018.

Sigmundsdottir, Alda. *The Little Book of the Hidden People: Twenty Stories of Elves from Icelandic Folklore*. Reykjavik: Little Books Publishing, 2015.

Simek, Rudolf. *Dictionary of Northern Mythology*. Translated by Angela Hall. Woodbridge, UK: D. S. Brewer, 2007.

Singh, Prerna. "How Biological Determinism Perpetuates Sexism Using 'Science.'" Feminism in India. June 18, 2018. https://feminisminindia.com /2018/06/18/biological-determinism-science-sexism/.

Smyser, H. M. "Ibn Fadlan's Account of the Rus with Some Commentary and Some Allusions to Beowulf." In *Franciplegius: Medieval and Linguistic Studies in Honor of Francis Peabody Magoun Jr.*, 92–119. Edited by Jess B. Bessinger Jr. and Robert P. Creed. New York: New York University Press, 1965.

Solly, Meilan. "Researchers Reaffirm Remains in Viking Warrior Tomb Belonged to a Woman." *Smithsonian*, February 21, 2019. https://www .smithsonianmag.com/smart-news/researchers-reaffirm-famed-ancient -viking-warrior-was-biologically-female-180971541.

———. "What Ötzi the Iceman's Tattoos Reveal about Copper Age Medical Practices." *Smithsonian*, September 10, 2018. https://www.smithsonian

mag.com/smart-news/what-otzi-icemans-tattoos-reveal-about-copper-age
-medical-practices-180970244/.

Sommer, Bettina Sejbjerg. "The Norse Concept of Luck." *Scandinavian Studies*
79, no. 3 (fall 2007): 275–94. https://www.jstor.org/stable/40920756.

Strapagiel, Lauren. "That 'Starter Witch Kit' Was Canceled After Massive
Backlash on Social Media." BuzzFeed News. September 6, 2018. https://
www.buzzfeednews.com/article/laurenstrapagiel/sephora-starter-witch
-kit-pinrose-white-sage.

Sturluson, Snorri. *The Heimskringla*. Translated by Samuel Laing. N.p.: Andesite Press, 2015.

———. *The Prose Edda: Norse Mythology*. Translated and edited by Jesse L. Byock. New York: Penguin Books, 2005.

Taylor, Kate. "Thousands of Americans Are Going to Church in Dead Malls."
Business Insider. June 19, 2017. https://www.businessinsider.com/dying
-malls-are-being-transformed-into-churches-2017-6.

Viking Archeology. "Ockelbo Runestone." Accessed June 13, 2022. http://
viking.archeurope.info/index.php?page=ockelbo-runestone.

Ward, Christie. "Valkyries, Wish-Maidens, and Swan-Maids." Viking Answer
Lady. Accessed November 1, 2022. http://www.vikinganswerlady.com
/valkyrie.shtml.

Wilkerson, Emily. "Writing the History of the Digital Revolution." Tulane
University. January 30, 2019. https://liberalarts.tulane.edu/newsletter
/writing-history-digital-revolution.

World English Bible. Edited by Michael Paul Johnson. Buena Vista, CO: Rainbow Missions, 2000.

INDEX

To Write to the Author

If you wish to contact the author or would like more information about this book, please write to the author in care of Llewellyn Worldwide Ltd. and we will forward your request. Both the author and the publisher appreciate hearing from you and learning of your enjoyment of this book and how it has helped you. Llewellyn Worldwide Ltd. cannot guarantee that every letter written to the author can be answered, but all will be forwarded. Please write to:

Ryan Smith
℅ Llewellyn Worldwide
2143 Wooddale Drive
Woodbury, MN 55125-2989
Please enclose a self-addressed stamped envelope for reply,
or $1.00 to cover costs. If outside the U.S.A., enclose
an international postal reply coupon.

Many of Llewellyn's authors have websites with additional information and resources. For more information, please visit our website at http://www.llewellyn.com.